FOR

DUMMIES®

PORTABLE EDITION

by Joyce Lain Kennedy and Lois-Andrea Ferguson

A John Wiley and Sons, Ltd, Publication

CVs For Dummies, Portable Edition

Published by
John Wiley & Sons, Ltd
The Atrium
Southern Gate
Chichester
West Sussex
PO19 8SQ
England

Email (for orders and customer service enquires): cs-books@wiley.co.uk

Visit our Home Page on www.wiley.com

For general information on our other products and services, please contact our Customer Care Department within the U.S. at 877-762-2974, outside the U.S. at 317-572-3993, or fax 317-572-4002.

For technical support, please visit www.wiley.com/techsupport.

Wiley also publishes its books in a variety of electronic formats. Some content that appears in print may not be available in electronic books.

British Library Cataloguing in Publication Data: A catalogue record for this book is available from the British Library

ISBN: 978-1-119-97438-3 (pbk), 978-1-119-97505-2 (ebk), 978-1-119-97506-9 (ebk), 978-1-119-97507-6 (ebk)

Printed and bound in Great Britain

10 9 8 7 6 5 4 3 2 1

WILEY

About the Authors

Joyce Lain Kennedy is America's first nationally syndicated careers columnist. Her twice-weekly column, CAREERS NOW, appears in newspapers and websites across the land. In her four decades of advising readers – young, old and in-between – Joyce has received millions of letters enquiring about career moves and jobs searches, and has answered countless numbers of them in print.

Joyce is the author of seven career books.

Lois-Andrea Ferguson is Managing Director of Professional CV Services Ltd and Senior Consultant / Developer for www.professional-cv-services.co.uk. Like many readers, Lois has switched careers over the last 20 years: from being an international journalist and writer to legal advisor on Privy Council issues, then professional fund-raising, securing more than £15 million for various community sector groups, then into the recruitment and selection sector.

Lois-Andrea has also conducted interviews with people such as former US President, George Bush Senior, and former US Secretary of State, Colin Powell. She had the memorable privilege of interviewing Dr Rob McNain, an astronaut who, two weeks after the interview, sadly died in the *Challenger* explosion. Lois has also contributed to BBC World Services and published short stories in North America and the UK.

Authors' Acknowledgements

Any book is a collaborative effort and I owe applause to a variety of people who guided me through a challenging process: Kathryn Troutman, Sarah Blazucki, James M. Lemke, John S. Gill, Traci Cumbay and Kelly James.

JLK

Thanks to Erglin and Leila Ferguson; Dr Sybil Wilson; Bobby, Yannic and Makeba McKoy; Emile, Eyton and Judy Ferguson.

LF

Publisher's Acknowledgements

We're proud of this book; please send us your comments through our Dummies online registration form located at www.dummies.com/register/.

Some of the people who helped bring this book to market include the following:

Acquisitions, Editorial and Media Development

Commissioning Editor: Wejdan Ismail

Assistant Editor: Ben Kemble

Production Manager: Daniel Mersey

Project Editor: Rachael Chilvers

Development Editor: Kelly Ewing

Technical Editor: Angela Baron, CIPD

Proofreader: David Price

Cover Photo: © iStock / Anne-Louise Quarfoth

Cartoons: Ed McLachlan

Composition Services

Project Coordinator: Kristie Rees

Layout and Graphics: Julie Trippetti

Proofreaders: John Greenough, Rebecca Denoncour, Jessica Kramer

Indexer: Potomac Indexing, LLC

Contents at a Glance

Introduction 1

Part 1: Pitching Your CV in a Fierce
Marketplace 5
Chapter 1: The Generic CV Is Past Its Sell-By Date 7
Chapter 2: Quick Online Ways to Find the Right Jobs 19
Chapter 3: Spotlighting Your CV in a Web 2.0 World 31
Chapter 4: Familiar Search Tools That Aren't Quite Dormant 39

Part 11: The Rise and Reign
of the Targeted CV 55
Chapter 5: Creating Your Best CV 57
Chapter 6: Flowing Content Versus Jarring Detail 77
Chapter 7: Words That Make the Mark 89
Chapter 8: Catching the Eye in Three Seconds Flat 109
Chapter 9: CVs for Your Life's Changing Phases 117
Chapter 10: Nabbing a Job as a New Graduate 129
Chapter 11: The Bare Essentials of a Cover Letter 145

Part 111: Bringing It All Together:
Sample Targeted CVs 155
Chapter 12: Targeted CVs by Industry and Career Field 157
Chapter 13: Targeted CVs by Experience Level and Age 165
Chapter 14: Targeted CVs for Special Circumstances 175

Part 1V: Launching Your CV Into Orbit 185
Chapter 15: References Authenticate Your CV 187
Chapter 16: Following Up on Your CV 195
Chapter 17: Almost Got the Interview Date? Prepare Yourself 211

Part V: The Part of Tens 217
Chapter 18: More than Ten Ways to Prove Your Claims 219
Chapter 19: Ten Ways to Improve Your CV 223
Chapter 20: Ten Things that Annoy Recruiters 229
Chapter 21: Your Ten-Point CV Checklist 235

Index 241

Contents

Introduction **1**

    About This Book 1
    Foolish Assumptions 2
    How This Book Is Organised 2
        Part I: Pitching Your CV in a Fierce Marketplace 2
        Part II: The Rise and Reign of the Targeted CV............ 3
        Part III: Bringing It All Together:
            Sample Targeted CVs 3
        Part IV: Launching Your CV Into Orbit......................... 3
        Part V: The Parts of Tens... 3
    Icons Used in This Book... 3
    Where to Go from Here 4

Part 1: Pitching Your CV in a Fierce Marketplace **5**

    Chapter 1: The Generic CV Is Past Its Sell-By Date 7

        In a New Era, the Targeted CV Rules....................................... 7
        Market Forces Zap Unqualified CVs 9
            Why mass posting of online CVs doesn't work.......... 10
            Enter Web 2.0 10
            Submitting your CV in a Web. 2.0 world 11
        Three Steps to Writing a Targeted CV................................. 12
        Sample Core CV and Spin-Offs.. 13
            Lauren's core CV.. 14
            Lauren's targeted CV... 14

    Chapter 2: Quick Online Ways to Find the Right Jobs. 19

        Climbing the Ladder: Vertical Job Search Engines.............. 20
            Searching the web for jobs.. 20
            Using a vertical: The generic basics............................ 22
            Meeting the verticals... 23
               SimplyHired.co.uk... 23
               Indeed.co.uk.. 24
        Job Boards Rising 25

The Continuing Power of Newspapers 27
  But here's the rest of the story 27
  A new wind is blowing on newspapers 28
Hunting on Company Websites 28
Seeking and Finding Is Easier than Ever 30

Chapter 3: Spotlighting Your CV in a Web 2.0 World 31

Making Something Happen with Web 2.0 Sites 31
Getting Involved in Online Social Networking.................... 33
  What it is 33
  Ways to get started.. 34
Writing about Jobs and Life: Blogs 36
  What it is 36
  Ways to get started.. 36
Receiving Live Feeds through Really Simple
  Syndication (RSS)... 37
  What it is 38
  Ways to get started.. 38

Chapter 4: Familiar Search Tools
That Aren't Quite Dormant. 39

Scannable CVs: Same as Ever 39
Plain Text CVs: A Long Last Gasp 42
  Converting your CV to plain text (ASCII).................... 43
  Avoiding ASCII landmines... 44
E-Forms: Filling in the Blankety-Blanks 46
The Fully Designed, Eye-Catching CV Is Back! 47
From Identity Theft to Recruiter Turn-Off:
  Why CV Blasting Is a Bad Idea 48
  Privacy and identity theft problems 49
  Overexposure to recruiters....................................... 50
Online Screening Keeps On Keepin' On 50
  Sample components of online screening.................... 51
  Pros and cons of online screening 53
  Can your CV be turned away?.................................... 53
Match Your CVs to the Jobs 54

Part II: The Rise and Reign of the Targeted CV..... 55

Chapter 5: Creating Your Best CV. 57

'Telling It' Mutes; 'Selling It' Sings.................................... 57
Focusing Your CV.. 59

CV Formats Make a Difference 61

The standard (reverse chronological) format 62

Strengths and weaknesses 64

Who can use this format and
who needs to think twice 64

Creating a standard (reverse
chronological) CV 65

The targeted format 66

Strengths and weaknesses 66

Who can use this format and
who needs to think twice 67

Creating a targeted CV 68

Executive format 68

Who can use this format and
who needs to think twice 68

Creating an executive CV 69

Academic curriculum vitae 70

Strengths and weaknesses 70

Who can use this format and
who needs to think twice 70

Creating an academic curriculum vitae 70

Making Contact with a Speculative Letter 74

Highlighting Your Best Work with a Portfolio 75

Choosing the Approach That Works for You 76

Chapter 6: Flowing Content Versus Jarring Detail 77

Exploring the Sections of Your CV 77

Leading with Contact Details 78

Including a Hook: Your Key Skills 80

Making Education and Experience Work for You 82

Education 82

Experience 82

Including Competencies 83

Gaining Extra Points 84

Activities 85

Organisations 85

Honours and awards 86

Licences and work samples 86

Shaping Your Content on Application Forms 87

Content to Omit: Your Salary Story 88

Chapter 7: Words That Make the Mark 89

Using Words to Bring Good News 89

Buzz words for administration and management 90

Buzz words for maximum effect 91

Buzz words for sales and persuasion..........................92
Buzz words for technical ability 93
Buzz words for office support.....................................94
Buzz words for teaching 95
Buzz words for research and analysis 96
Buzz words for helping and care work 97
Buzz words for financial management.......................98
Buzz words for many skills..99
Unlocking Your Talents with Keywords 100
Keywords for administration/management 102
Keywords for banking..102
Keywords for customer service.................................103
Keywords for information technology......................103
Keywords for manufacturing......................................104
Keywords for human resources.................................104
Knowing Where to Find Keywords 105
Getting a Grip on Grammar...106
Spelling Like a Pro...108

Chapter 8: Catching the Eye in Three Seconds Flat ... 109

Word Processing in a Nutshell...110
Printing Your CV 111
Selecting Paper..112
Being Consistent 113
Breaking It Up 114
Choosing Typefaces and Font Size 115

Chapter 9: CVs for Your Life's Changing Phases 117

Grabbing Good Jobs When You're Older............................117
The strengths of maturity..118
The mature person's soft spots 119
A lower-level job beckons..121
Employment in the autumn years 123
Winning Interviews as a New Civilian.................................124
Making military strengths count.................................124
Dealing with military soft spots 125
Government Hopefuls: From Private to Public 126

Chapter 10: Nabbing a Job as a New Graduate......129

Getting Your Foot in the Door...129
Revising and Drafting Your CV..130
Case Study: Landing the Job with Experience 133

Case Studying: Nabbing the Job When
You Have No Experience.. 136
Wading through the Maze of Graduate
Application Forms.. 137
Facing the harsh reality 138
Getting your mind in gear.. 138
Moving into the maze of questions and answers 139
Wrapping up this competency-based
question maze 143

Chapter 11: The Bare Essentials of a Cover Letter 145

Why Cover Letters Are Important 145
Getting Started with Definitions... 146
Writing the Cover Letter 148
Opening salutations.. 148
The body... 149
Closing salutations 150
Checking Out Cover Letter Examples................................. 150

**Part III: Bringing It All Together:
Sample Targeted CVs....................................... 155**

**Chapter 12: Targeted CVs by Industry
and Career Field 157**

Targeted CV for IT or Management 157
Targeted CV for Medicine 159
Targeted CV for Engineering 162

**Chapter 13: Targeted CVs by Experience
Level and Age 165**

School-Leaver with No Work Experience........................... 165
Graduate with Some Experience... 166
Management CV 166
Senior Executive CV... 166

**Chapter 14: Targeted CVs for Special
Circumstances..175**

Changing a Qualified Teacher's CV for Jobs
in Education and Management...................................... 175
Creating Specialist CVs 178
Targeting Community Sector and Medical Positions........ 179

Part IV: Launching Your CV Into Orbit............ 185

Chapter 15: References Authenticate Your CV 187
The Harm Caused by a So-So Reference 187
Seven Things You Need to Do about References............. 188
Ban references from your CV..................................... 189
Expect employers to check references..................... 189
Choose references with thought 190
Help references help you.. 190
Play safe with a reference folder 191
Stamp out bad references.. 191
Thank everyone 193
Finding References without Shedding
Your Cloak of Secrecy 193
Allow Enough Time for Skilful Reference Management 194

Chapter 16: Following Up on Your CV 195
Follow-Up Efforts Are Essential 195
Questions to Ask Yourself Before Following Up 197
Do I phone or email my follow-up?........................... 197
What powerful opening statement can I make?....... 198
How much information can I find out
from a central phone operator?............................... 198
How can I get past gate-keepers?.............................. 199
What can I do with voicemail? 201
Why shouldn't I leave a message asking
the target to call me back?...................................... 202
How can I keep track of my follow ups?................... 202
When is it time to throw in the towel?...................... 203
Monitoring Your Follow-up Efforts 203
Using the Follow-Up Matrix 204
Factors on the Follow-Up Matrix................. 205
The Values Key... 206
Checking out a sample Matrix.................................... 208
Fast-Tracking Your Successful Follow-Up........................ 208

Chapter 17: Almost Got the Interview Date?
Prepare Yourself............................... 211
When Your Job Conflicts with an Interview Date 212
Face-to-Face Beats Ear-to-Ear.. 212
Going Overboard on Ardour Can Cost You Money 213
When the Interview Is Out of Town 213
Making the Most of Your Moment 214

Part V: The Part of Tens 217

Chapter 18: More than Ten Ways to Prove Your Claims 219

Say It with Numbers.. 220
Say It with Percentages 221
Say It with Amounts in Pounds 222

Chapter 19: Ten Ways to Improve Your CV 223

Match Your CV to the Job.. 223
Use Bulleted Style for Easy Reading 223
Discover the Art of Lost Articles.. 224
Sell, Don't Tell.. 224
Show Off Your Assets 225
Make Sure Your Words Play Well Together 225
Reach Out with Strength... 226
Avoid a Weak Skills Profile 226
Check Out the Technology 226
Erase the 'Leave-Outs'.. 227

Chapter 20: Ten Things that Annoy Recruiters.......229

CV-Free Pitches 229
Major Mismatches 229
E-Stalking... 230
Missing Caps and Typos 231
Too Much Information 232
Date Grate 232
Guess Who 233
File Style 233
Useless and Uninformative 234
Probable Prevarication 234

Chapter 21: Your Ten-Point CV Checklist 235

Matching Skills for Skills 235
Format and Style 236
Focus and Image... 236
Achievements and Skills 236
Language and Expressions 236
Content and Omissions 237
Length and Common Sense 237
Appearance: Online Attached and Paper CVs..................... 237

Difficult Issues and Sugar-coating 238
Proofreading and More Proofreading 238
The Power of Targeted CVs 238

Index 241

Introduction

*T*ake a trip down memory lane, to 20 years ago, when CV writing was so simple and straightforward. Those were the days when you scoured the dailies for job advertisements, sent your CV on plain paper, stating your name, your address and more often than not, your land line number along with your employment and education history. Then you listened out for the telephone to ring for an interview.

Today the journey is more hurried, with lots of clicks and the electronic voice 'You have email!' Sometimes, you no longer only send your CV through the post. You sit at the computer, uploading your targeted CVs, filling in countless agency forms and contributing to a massive database which picks up key words you've had the insight to include. Then you await an offer of an interview perhaps via email or text.

About This Book

Getting to grips with the modern world of recruitment means figuring out the difference between the scannable CV and the Internet plain text CV (ASCII). Relax – there's also the tried and proven traditional CV which is formatted for employers to read in their hands, not by flicking down a scrollbar.

In this book, we explain the way CVs work in today's hi-tech world without saturating your brain with science. We hope this book will be a vital tool for all job-hunters, from young school-leavers struggling with a blank CV, all the way through to the senior professor writing a document to avoid being a victim of ageism. Whatever your circumstances, we tell you everything you need to know to create a targeted CV.

In these pages, we demonstrate how to scale the fence of success with hard-hitting advice to enhance your confidence and make you stand out amongst the hopefuls. A fierce labour market is out there. But flip the pages at your own pace and gain invaluable tools for your journey to those employers' doors!

Foolish Assumptions

We assume you picked up this book for one of the following reasons:

- You like where you are today but want more from life than blooming where you're planted.

- You've heard about sweeping technology-based changes in the way people and jobs find each other. You want to be sure your CV is in sync with the very latest updates.

- You're a school-leaver venturing into the labour market for the first time and want an experienced, friendly hand on your shoulder.

- You're a recent graduate with a little bit of experience seeking clarification between the CV and application form process.

- You're a parent who's nurtured children for years and is ready to return to the workplace but needs to know what's changed.

- You're a manager or senior director wanting to climb the next rung on the corporate ladder and know it's time for a CV makeover.

We further assume that you're someone who likes information that cuts to the chase, sometimes with a smile.

How This Book Is Organised

The aim of this book is get you up and running (which in this case means happily employed) as soon as possible. This book is divided into five distinct parts and each part is divided into chapters. Here's the break-down on what each part covers.

Part 1: Pitching Your CV in a Fierce Marketplace

This part covers the big picture trends and developments, and what you should do to make your CV stand out amongst the Web giants.

Part II: The Rise and Reign of the Targeted CV

This part shows you how to make your targeted CV hard-hitting to beat competitors to the employers' doors. We pay special attention to recognisable groups of people such as recent graduates, those who have vast experiences but worry about ageism, military personnel entering the civilian world and parents who want to resume work after bringing up children.

Part III: Bringing It All Together: Sample Targeted CVs

In this part we give you a sampling of targeted CVs for different circumstances, by industry and experience. We also explain ways of changing directions with the same CV contents.

Part IV: Launching Your CV Into Orbit

This part shows you how to use references to your advantage, successfully start your job campaign and prepare for that elusive interview.

Part V: The Parts of Tens

For Dummies readers know that the Part of Tens is a collection of single-subject chapters that cut to the chase in a ten-point format.

In these lists of ten, we offer ways to back up your CV claims, identify actions to avoid driving recruiters barmy, suggest simple adjustments to quickly improve your CV, and give you a CV checklist to rate your work.

Icons Used in This Book

We use *For Dummies* signature icons in the margins of the book to rivet your attention on key bits of information.

People have differing opinions about certain aspects of CV writing and recruitment. The gavel reminds you to make the best decision for your situation.

This icon directs your attention to great techniques to create a winning CV.

The knotted string alerts you to the really important points to remember.

Head here for information that can make a difference in the outcome of your job search.

This icon warns you avoid certain pitfalls that can reduce your chances in securing that job.

Where to Go from Here

You can start anywhere you want to in this book – each chapter stands alone so you can flip through to different sections as you like, using the Table of Contents and Index to pinpoint the most useful information for you. To be in tune with current standards and practices, go to Part I. If you're writing your first CV, the chapters in Part II offers worksheets, words to make your CV sing and tips on how to present your CV for instant attention from the employer. Want to see a selection of sample CVs? Head to Part III.

Otherwise, jump in where the topic and samples look inviting and applicable – we've done our best to make it all outstanding.

Part I
Pitching Your CV in a Fierce Marketplace

'Being a pretty boy, able to peel grapes, and a good talker with flying experience would have made the perfect cabin steward, but it would have saved us <u>both</u> a lot of time if you'd sent in a photograph, Mr Joseph.'

In this part . . .

You find trends and developments impacting your CV that you absolutely, positively must know about to remain competitive in the whirling landscape that is recruitment today. This part presents easy understanding of the best CV moves in an era of technology transition.

Chapter 1

The Generic CV Is Past Its Sell-By Date

• •

In This Chapter

▶ Understanding the radical change overtaking CVs

▶ Writing targeted CVs

▶ Fighting back when technology isn't your friend

• •

*W*elcome to our book. If your job search isn't going well even though you've submitted dozens of CVs, then you're in the right chapter. In this chapter, we offer new insight for you with a quick update on how to thrive in a landscape where recruiting processes have turned digital but CV practices are stuck in analogue.

In a New Era, the Targeted CV Rules

At some point in a hunt for better employment, everyone needs market-driven job search communications. That is, everyone needs a CV or something very much like a CV that comprises the following elements:

▸ Your contact details

▸ A summary of your current, most recent and past employment

▸ Your education, training, awards, achievements or affiliations

Personal information about your nationality, how many children you have and marital status is discouraged.

The CV tells the buyer (employer) these types of critical facts:

- ✔ Why you're an excellent match for the job
- ✔ What skills you'll bring to the organisation
- ✔ Why you're worth the money you hope to earn
- ✔ Your capacity for doing the work better than other candidates
- ✔ Your ability to solve company or industry problems

However, conquering the job market is getting trickier and requires more effort than the last time you baited your hook. Even if you were job hunting fairly recently, CVs and related techniques that were revolutionary in the savvy jobseeker's toolkit 12 years ago are headed for ancient history. *The generic CV is at the top of the list of job search tools nearing extinction.*

This almost-extinct generic format charts your employment history in reverse chronological order, as most CVs do. Many people make the mistake of cramming everything in with the hope that the employer will pick up on the relevant data for the positions they seek, no matter if the employer finds this information on the third page!

In modern recruitment, employers don't have time to wade through pages of detail. In steps the *targeted CV*. This format specifically places relevant information to the fore. For example, if you insert a Key Skills box at the top of the first page, make sure to emphasise those skills relevant to the position you seek. Employers will scan the box first and begin short-listing you as their eye moves down the page.

If you have a generic CV lying around in a desk drawer somewhere and are tempted to use it, don't! Although a generic CV casts a wide net to snag the attention of many employers – and saves time for those who are too busy getting through the day to keep writing different CVs for different jobs – it's not effective in a fierce and competitive market with e-databases that search with ferocity for those 'key' words.

A targeted CV is a marketing tool that convinces the reader that your work will benefit a specific employer and that you should make the short list cut of candidates invited in for a closer look.

Unlike a generic CV, a targeted CV format:

- ✔ Addresses a given opportunity, making it easy to see how your qualifications are a close match to a job's requirements.

- ✔ Uses powerful words to persuade and a clean design to attract interest.

- ✔ Plays up strengths and downplays any factor that undermines your bid for an interview.

Industry consultants observe that companies are weary of sifting through too many CVs and instead will substitute e-CVs, screening questions via the web, and assessment instruments (tests) in deciding who gets offered a job interview.

Market Forces Zap Unqualified CVs

The word got out, slowly at first. And then – whoosh! – millions of jobseekers found out how easy it is, thanks to the Internet, to instantly put a CV in the hands of employers across the country as well as across town. *Post and pray* became the jobseekers' mantra as they learned how to manipulate online CVs and click them into the digital world as quickly as fast-shuffling dealers lay down cards at casino poker tables.

The move toward mass posting of CVs online began back in the first phase of the World Wide Web, which retroactively is termed *Web 1.0*, a time frame of about 1994 to 2005.

But the Net's CV sludge got yuckier and more frustrating when commercial CV-blasting services appeared on the scene. Almost overnight, it seemed, anyone willing to pay the price could scatter CV confetti everywhere an online address could be found.

Why mass posting of online CVs doesn't work

The consequences of CV spamming for employers were staggering: Despite their use of the Web 1.0 era's best recruiting selection software, employers were overrun with unsolicited, disorganised generic CVs containing everything but DNA details.

And what about the jobseekers who sent all those wonderful generic, unstructured CVs? They were left to wonder in disappointment why they never got a call back.

It's all in the numbers. A job advertised by a major company in the era before Web 1.0 may have attracted hundreds or even thousands of responses, but the same ad posted online creates a feeding frenzy of many thousands of CVs. A few super-sized companies report that they receive millions of unsolicited CVs each year. No wonder the web is overwhelmed with billions of CVs that overwhelm both technology and eyeballs. No wonder employment databases are hammered with such mismatches as sales clerks and sports trainers applying for jobs as scientists and senior managers, and vice versa.

Enter Web 2.0

Fast-forward to when digital curtains went up on a second Internet phase. It's called *Web 2.0,* a term suggesting a host of new ideas and amazing software that has leapt onto the world recruiting stage. Web 2.0 is fuelled by the desire of companies to eliminate CV fatigue and, at the same time, to outdo the competition in acquiring top talent. And, of course, employers universally want to do it better, faster, cheaper.

Briefly, the web-based services of Web 2.0 are characterised by their movement away from static, rigid websites that merely list jobs and links by which to apply for them and towards richer, more interactive and socially inclusive methods. (To read more about Web 2.0 services, check out Chapters 2 and 3.)

To clone or not to clone? Mirroring ad language

Must you use the exact words in the job ad? Two schools of thought exist on this question. Some authorities advise that you should state your qualifications in the identical language used in the ad to which you respond. The ditto contingent points out that computer selection software awards rating points to a CV based on how closely your words mirror those in the job ad: Get closer to the ad, get more points.

Others disagree, saying that modern recruiting software is sophisticated enough to grasp your qualifications even though you use synonyms and related terms and not the exact same words.

As employers hope to use Web 2.0 solutions to dry out the CV deluge created by Web 1.0 innovation, jobseekers have updated aspirations as well. In Web 1.0, jobseekers wanted to know how to *get onto* the Internet. In Web 2.0, jobseekers want to know how to *get noticed* on the Internet.

Submitting your CV in a Web. 2.0 world

Market forces, the term describing the interaction of supply and demand that shapes a market economy, are pulling companies towards targeted CVs by rewarding them with less unnecessary work to wade through. And market forces are pulling jobseekers towards targeted CVs by showing them how to get noticed on the Internet.

Following are the vital rules to submitting your CV in Web 2.0:

- ✔ Make sure to read the ad properly and follow instructions as to how to apply. You can cut and paste the duties you've carried out from one targeted CV to another but work on the Key Skills section (see Chapter 6) to make the contents specific to the job you're applying for.

- ✔ Make sure to also put your matching qualifications. You may consider leading off your Key Skills with the most relevant one. For example, if the job requires someone with qualifications in Sales and you have a degree in Marketing, this is very relevant.

✔ Keep your CV current. The classic tip to stay at the top of a list of candidates by changing a word or two in your CV and re-posting to recruitment agencies is alive and well.

Three Steps to Writing a Targeted CV

When you're beginning to think seriously about greener grass, the race is on! You already need 36-hour days to accomplish all the responsibilities you carry on your shoulders. And then you see a job that you hope has your name on it but you can't carve out the time to write from scratch a targeted CV that will show an employer why you're the one to interview.

Your answer is to begin building a core CV before the pressure hits, using it as a basis for targeted editions when you must move quickly. Constructing a targeted CV is easier when you follow this game plan:

1. **Prepare your core CV.**

   Your core CV is, in fact, a rough draft of factual details you store for later targeting. Probe your memory to jot down every factor in your background – from experience, competencies and skills to education – that you can use to customise a CV. This core CV is your working model, a document you never submit to an employer but a drawer full of vital data that you can pull out over and over again. Use as many pages as you need.

2. **Research requirements of job.**

   If you're responding to a specific advertised job, jot down the requirements that the ad lists. Don't confuse the job duties and the stated requirements. Deal first with the requirements and then see how you can show experience or education that matches the most important job duties.

   When you're not responding to a specific advertised job but are posting your CV in an online database, attempt to attract interest in your candidacy by

researching the most commonly requested qualifications for a given occupation or career field. You can
do this by studying many job ads.

3. **Customise each spin-off CV.**

   After compiling the requirements, you must satisfy
   them in a tailor-made CV. Scour your core document
   to see whether you can add secondary items mentioned in the ad that further improve your chances,
   and start writing.

   A way to cut down on your time and effort is by
   customising just part of each CV. In constructing a
   two-page CV, customise the first page and, whenever
   possible, keep the second page the same each time.
   Freezing the second page isn't always possible, but
   the concept is a good starting point.

Some people assume the CV has to be laid out on one page.
Wrong. Modern employers realise that people move around
from one job to another, change careers and sometimes
include information on projects and achievements. Presenting
your CV on two pages or, where appropriate, more, is better
than to mercilessly edit content down to one page and lose
detail.

Sample Core CV and Spin-Offs

Look over the following examples for (fictional) Lauren
Simpson. You can see how attention to detail can make all the
difference in getting your CV noticed, first by computers and
then by humans.

After leaving secondary school, Lauren worked for a year
as administrative assistant at a health insurance company.
Deciding she didn't want to continue in administrative work,
Lauren landed a job as a sales assistant at a High Street wom-
en's wear chain.

She was good at retailing, and after six months, the cloth-
ing chain offered her a managerial traineeship at one store.
Once there, Lauren enrolled in an internal Retail Management
course and while working and studying, she was promoted to
assistant manager.

A few years later, Lauren joined another retail company and she has now decided to change careers. Although going back to education and re-training for another career field is an option Lauren is considering, she isn't anxious to incur student debt. Before doing that, she's checking out how she can adapt her hard-earned experience to related work such as Sales Management or Marketing.

Lauren's core CV

Using a reverse chronological time frame (see Chapter 5), Lauren writes a comprehensive document, highlighting her competencies, skills and accomplishments (see Figure 1-1). Lauren creates distinct units that she can add and subtract as needed when she targets a specific position.

Lauren's targeted CV

Spotting an ad for a sales position with a company that markets products through beauty salons, Lauren takes note of the requirements:

1 Experience in sales and/or marketing management

2 Practical knowledge of shop floor operations and merchandising

3 Ability to motivate multi-tasked teams and achieve results

4 Relevant qualifications in retail and associated industries

5 Extensive skills in designing customer relations strategies

Here's how Lauren addresses each of cosmetic's company requirements:

✔ Requirement 1 shows up in the skills summary and under management duties at LouAnn's.

✔ Requirement 2 is addressed by her merchandising co-ordinator duty at LouAnn's.

✔ Requirement 3 appears as a management skill at LouAnn's.

✔ Requirement 4 is met under the education segment. Note that Lauren spells out her retail merchandising studies because the salons job requires a familiarity with what retail customers will buy.

✔ Requirement 5 is noted in two places. The first is a subheading titled 'Customer Relations Management' at LouAnn's. The second is also at LouAnn's, within the Accomplishments segment.

Lauren L. Simpson

LouAnn's
Based in London, LouAnn's is a division of Goodwear, FAS, with garments marketed to professional women in 220 stores across the UK.

(Date)	Assistant Manager, New Bond Street, London
(Date)	Sales Assistant and Manager-in-Training, Oxford Circus
(Date)	Sales Assistant, Milton Keynes

Sales and Business Analysis
- Maximised merchandise visibility by analysing customer traffic patterns.
- Set effective work schedules by analysing store sales.

Customer Relations Management
- Developed 16 high-spending customers by forging relations.
- Sold by appointment where possible.

Management
- Communicated via phone and consulted with corporate management daily.
- Met national goals and competed with all UK stores for daily sales results.
- Supervised two to three part-time sales reps on each shift.
- Trained employees how best to utilise the selling system.
- Worked with floor plans to display merchandise for maximum sales.
- Met daily management responsibilities, maintaining sales floor, inventory, shipping, ordering and record-keeping. Keyboard 40 WMP, competent use of Microsoft Suite, including Word, Excel, Outlook and PowerPoint.

Accomplishments
- Personally delivered one-third of overall store revenue closing 30,000 to 40,000 sales per month in store with 7 staff (3 full-time and 4 part-time).
- Consistently maximised income through commissions earned.
- In three months averaged £15,000 per month sales from regular customers.

OTHER EXPERIENCE
(Date)   Blue Arrow, Kent
County office of health insurance company

Administrative Assistant
- After secondary school, worked one year in administration for government marketing department.
- Compiled marketing analysis and supported cross-company project teams.

EDUCATION
(Date)   BA, Retail Merchandising
Leeds University

Figure 1-1: A core CV is a comprehensive document.

Lauren purposely did not include certain information, such as her job right after secondary school as an administrative assistant at a health insurance company, because it isn't relevant to the position she seeks. Usually, you can leave jobs out if they're more than 10 years old and irrelevant to the position you're applying to. However, if they are relevant to the position, you include them.

Lauren L. Simpson

Accomplishments
- The HR Director complimented me on creating the model for a quarterly newsletter, on my creativity and for my presentation of company values.
- After six months of assisting buyer in making presentations to store personnel, I facilitate 35 stores on my own.

LouAnn's
Based in London, LouAnn's is a division of Goodwear, FAS, with garments marketed to professional women in 220 stores across the UK.

(Date)	Assistant Manager, New Bond Street, London
(Date)	Sales Assistant and Manager-in-Training, Marley Bourne
(Date)	Sales Assistant, Milton Keynes

Sales and Business Analysis
- Maximised merchandise visibility by analysing customer traffic patterns.
- Set effective work schedules by analysing each employee's sales as well as store sales.

Customer Relations Management
- Developed 16 high-spending customers by forging relations with new ones.
- Sold by appointment where possible.

Management
- Communicated via phone and consulted with corporate management daily.
- Met national goals and competed with stores in UK for daily sales results.
- Supervised two to three part-time sales reps on each shift.
- Trained employees how best to utilise selling system.
- Worked with floor plans to display merchandise for maximum sales.
- Maintained sales floor, inventory, shipping, ordering and record-keeping.
Word, Excel, Outlook and PowerPoint.

OTHER EXPERIENCE
(Date)   Blue Arrow, Kent
County office of health insurance company

Administrative Assistant
- One year in administration for government marketing department.
- Compiled marketing analysis and supported cross-company project teams.

EDUCATION
(Date)   BA, Retail Merchandising
Leeds University

Figure 1-2: Spin-off A addresses each of the ad's requirements.

Here's how Lauren addresses the requirements from the ad placed by the health insurance company:

✔ Lauren meets requirement 1 in the education segment. Because the health insurance marketing job is not on the retail level, Lauren selects a few different facts from her core CV to those she chose for spin-off CV A. Lauren truthfully writes that she has a business degree and doesn't mention retail merchandising, part of her studies at the business school she attended.

If during an interview Lauren is asked about her studies in retail merchandising, Lauren will bypass the issue, briefly pointing out the plus factors in learning retail merchandising, and then moving onto her marketing and business coursework and her experience-based accomplishments.

✔ Lauren responds to requirement 2 with her marketing experience at Lou-Ann's.

✔ Requirement 3, knowledge of the health care industry, was more difficult to match than the other requirements but Lauren reaches back to the health insurance company she worked for right after secondary school.

✔ Lauren addresses requirement 4 in her opening summary of qualifications. A reading of her CV backs up her claims regarding leadership in a collaborative environment.

When you write your targeted CV, remember the magic formula:

Employer wants	*You offer*
A	A
B	B
C	C
D	D

To accomplish this custom-fit hiring, make your self-marketing document a targeted CV that convinces a single employer that your *value proposition* (a buzzword phrase meaning 'reason for employment') is a perfect fit for the job, not a *maybe* fit for the job.

When technology fails: the human antidote

When technology defeats you, consider alternative strategies that are most advantageous to you. Play on your turf. Get personal:

✔ Develop your own job leads by doing substantial research and targeting your CV for a direct application.

✔ Follow up on job ads, but to diffuse the crushing competition, attempt to figure out who the manager is and contact that decision maker directly (see Chapter 2). You can even write a CV letter (see Chapter 5) to that person, but do not mention the job ad. Your approach is that you've been researching companies where your excellent qualifications may be a good fit. Even if this 'happy coincidence' causes the manager to send your CV to the HR department, now it arrives from an important executive and is likely to be examined.

✔ Remember that the vast majority of jobs are found in small businesses. Many aren't yet using modern job-search tools and will value your person-to-person approach.

That is, meet as many of the employer's requirements as you truthfully can. Admittedly, doing so isn't a walk on the beach. Expect to do some head scratching and creative thinking from time to time in a world growing not only more global but more complex as the clock ticks.

Chapter 2

Quick Online Ways to Find the Right Jobs

. . . .

In This Chapter

▶ Using job search engines

▶ Reviewing media job ads

▶ Going directly to company websites

. . . .

*T*his book shows you how to master the New Era art of peppering each CV with persuasive marketing facts that target a job's requirements. Even if the job requirements and your qualifications are a perfect match, your efforts can go down the drain if you can't put your marketing facts before people who can employ you.

The Internet makes uncovering hoards of job opportunities easier than ever; the trick is to find the right ones for you. In this chapter, we discuss the online tools you can use to reach the right eyes without stumbling around and wasting time. First, we examine the really new tools and then we take an updated look at familiar resources.

One important note: The history of the past decade proves that recruiting technology changes constantly. That's why we cover this chapter's online job-hunt destinations as a digest, using relatively few examples to illustrate the concepts you want to know.

Climbing the Ladder: Vertical Job Search Engines

Vertical job search engines – also called *verticals*, *VJSEs* or *aggregators* – are the job seeker's new best friends, and they're changing the online recruitment game in dramatic ways. You can think of VJSEs as 'Google for jobs'. That is, the verticals work like Google or other search engines, except they search only for job listings.

Verticals represent the next level in job search and they've arrived in the nick of time for harried job seekers, who can use the services without cost.

In days of yore, you could grow old and grey wasting weeks trudging through job listing after job listing on various job boards. One informed guesstimate says there are 50,000 job boards around the world! By contrast to this crowded cyber-market, where you board-hop from one site to another and on and on, the cutting-edge job verticals offer one-stop job shopping.

Modern day hunter-gatherers, the verticals do the collection work for you, making it possible to go to one place and see virtually all the jobs on the Internet that fit your personal criteria. Verticals give you the options to slice and dice your search results, based on what you want, such as full- or part-time, large companies or small, and so on. And they reveal when each job was posted. Some verticals even show you where the jobs are clustered on a map.

Searching the web for jobs

Verticals use specialised search engines to *scrape* (crawl) the web to find and haul in job content. That is, they use automated programs (software) called *spiders* or *robots*. The '*bots* go sleuthing on the web, compiling a vast array of listings from newspaper classified ads, job boards, corporate sites, and industry associations.

The verticals also receive *online feeds* (direct communications) from job boards that want their listings included in a VJSE's inventory of jobs.

TIP

REMEMBER

Four signs of hot verticals

Even though VJSEs are gifts from the technology gods who know how busy you are, they're not all created the same. Whether you experiment with one vertical at a time, or arrange for relevant job listings to your computer from several verticals simultaneously and watch them compete for jobs that match your criteria, bear in mind the four basic requirements for a great experience. They are:

✔ Search-and-match technology that works correctly

✔ Wide coverage of available jobs with dates of postings

✔ Easy-to-use delivery options (email or RSS feeds; see Chapter 3)

✔ Tools for saving and managing saved searches

Based on the keywords you supply, you can bring all relevant listings to your computer in one search by using a vertical job search site.

The vertical sites usually don't engage in job transactions themselves but pass users along to the source of the information. The verticals can point you to speciality job recruiters you've never heard of but that are opportunity-rich for your occupation or industry.

While it's true that some of the material that vertical engines come up with also appears on large search engines (such as Google, Yahoo!, MSN, or Ask.com), the general-purpose engines lack the vertical engines' *relevancy* (the degree to which a job matches what you specified) or the ability to *filter* (sort out unwanted search results).

By contrast, job seekers using VJSEs can filter search results using a wealth of criteria. You may, for example, want to look at jobs at companies with annual revenues of more than 50 million pounds, or within 25 miles of a postcode, or only those jobs based on another criterion that you choose.

The biggest potential fly in the VJSE soup is what may happen when the new vertical giants do not have contractual agreements with the original publishers of job ads. Some verticals are attempting to index and post for free all the job openings in the universe, including those that employers paid to place on job boards, in print, and through other media. Whether potential legal squabbles will eventually cut into your one-stop convenience by shrinking the number of job postings you can shop on a VJSE is unknown. But for now and the foreseeable future, vertical job search sites are the hot new blood-hounds to help you sniff out the jobs you want.

Using a vertical: The generic basics

While each vertical search engine includes specific instructions on the best way to use it, you can expect certain basic information to apply across the board. Here are the general steps you're likely to follow when using a vertical search engine:

1. **Create a personal account.**

   Register with one or several verticals. Many job listings appear on all the verticals because, with exceptions, they take their content from the same places.

2. **Decide how to receive the jobs.**

   You may prefer daily or weekly job alerts. Or you may choose an RSS (real simple syndication) feed (Chapter 3) to have job ads sent as they are posted directly to your computer or hand-held device.

3. **Set preferences.**

   Use the preferences setting to select the jobs you want to appear on your results page. You may select to show results based only on location (postcodes) or timeliness, for example.

4. **Become familiar with related options on the vertical site.**

   Options vary by vertical but may include such extras as a map of the job's location, salary market information, company research, or potential contacts inside the target company.

5. **Narrow your search.**

   Drill down through the job listings to be as specific as possible to get to the jobs you want.

   Quality – not quantity – counts most. Look for freshness of the listing and those jobs that are relevant to your preferences. Search on skills, interests and location.

6. **Track and save your searches.**

   Each vertical allows you to save your searches on its site. Doing so enables you to manage the most current and desirable listings.

7. **Upgrade to advanced search, if you need it.**

   If you're drowning in job listings or seem to be missing the mark, try using the vertical's advanced search feature. You can search by such criteria as keywords, words in job title, company, type of job and location.

Meeting the verticals

Here's a thumbnail sketch of each of the best-known verticals, those that offer the most amenities and draw from thousands of sources. Expect the details of any or all of these sites to change from time to time.

SimplyHired.co.uk

Simply Hired is an award-winning site that says it's building the largest online database of jobs on the planet, indexed from large and small job boards, newspaper and classified listings, government and association websites, and company websites.

What about the power of whom you know? Simply Hired's business network partner LinkedIn offers a referral job network that aims to connect job applicants with recruitment managers. The 'Who Do I Know' button displays after each job listing to help you discover whether you have an 'inside friend' whom you can tap for referrals or information. The service has a similar partnership with the social networking site, MySpace.

Indeed.co.uk

In one simple search, Indeed gives job seekers free access to millions of jobs from thousands of websites. All the job listings from major job boards, newspaper classifieds, associations, and company career pages are included.

With the familiar look and feel of general search engines, the popular Indeed makes it easy to drill down by keyword and location to jobs that fit your requirements. You can quick-search from the Indeed home page. Just type keywords into the 'What' box describing the kind of job you want, and enter a city or postcode in the 'Where' box. Then click the 'Find Jobs' button or hit the Enter key on your keyboard.

You can put search results on your plate in several different ways. For example, you can

✔ View results ranked by relevance (how close the job comes to what you want).

✔ View results ranked by date, with newest jobs appearing first.

✔ View results by the distance of your potential commute to work.

Indeed's 'Advanced Job Search' allows for more sophisticated filtering. You can specify exact phrases, exclude jobs that contain certain keywords, exclude jobs from recruitment agencies, and limit results to jobs published today or within the last week.

There's more. When you want to research a company, investigate salaries for that kind of job, see who you may know at the company through networking sites like LinkedIn, or view the job's location on Google maps, click on the 'More Actions' link next to each job search result.

totaljobs.co.uk

One of the UK's most visited commercial recruitment websites, carrying more than 150,000 line vacancies at any one time. Part of Totaljobs Group Ltd, this is the UK's largest and fastest growing online recruitment company, comprising 10 recruitment websites which between them carry over 300,000 jobs, attract over 3.5 million unique jobseekers, and generate 2 million applications every month.

Reed.co.uk

Reed purports to be the UK's leading specialist recruitment and HR services provider, providing recruitment solutions to employers and jobseekers for over 46 years.

Reed offers HR and recruitment services to businesses of all sizes. The company was the first recruitment company to offer specialist recruitment services, beginning with the creation of Reed Accountancy in the 1960s. Since then, the company has continued to tailor its recruitment services, with 24 individual business specialisms offering recruitment solutions in distinct industry sectors. According to Reed, more than 2.5 million candidates are now registered on reed.co.uk, more than any other UK job site.

Job Boards Rising

Since 1994, when job boards effectively began operating in the then new recruiting terrain, it has seemed as though another one appears daily. Today, as noted earlier in this chapter, estimates put the number of job boards operating globally as high as 50,000.

If you've been in the job market during the past 15 years or so, you probably know that a *job board* is a website where you can look for a job. Employers pay job boards to post their open positions. Job seekers typically view their jobs for free.

You can apply through a job board for specific positions, or you can post your CV in the board's CV database. You can search for job listings by career field, occupation, job title, location, and job detail keywords. The emphasis is on local job markets because most people won't move for a job unless they have little choice.

Job boards haven't been frozen in time. They often add user-friendly enhancements, including privacy-sensitive features and quick matching of job situation and jobseeker.

Watch out for the black hole at major job boards

Recruiter Mary Nurrenbrock doesn't sugar-coat it when describing her view of the practice of responding to jobs advertised on the major job boards:

'When you respond to openings directly through job boards, your CV usually ends up in a black hole, a passive database. If you're responding right from the board, it's going to HR. Bad move. These guys are up to their eyeballs and usually don't even really know what the hiring manager is looking for. That is, if the HR person even sees the CV in the passive database.

'You need to get to the hiring manager, not HR. How? When you visit a job board and see a job that looks like it's a fit (you notice we didn't say that it looks interesting), go to that company's website and get a

name. Most of the corporate sites have profiles. Get the name of the VP Marketing, CEO, CMO – whomever the open position is likely to report to.

'Figuring out the address isn't hard. Look under the press releases where you'll usually find a company contact email address. Use the same format – john_smith@, john.smith@, jsmith@ – to send your CV. If it bounces back, try a different format. If that doesn't work, try to wrangle the address from the company receptionist. If all else fails, snail mail it.

'What usually happens next is that the hiring manager sends your CV to HR. But we're trying to avoid that, right? No, we're trying to avoid the black hole. Now the HR person is looking at a CV that came to her from an internal source. Big difference!'

You find job boards in two basic flavours:

- ✔ **General job boards,** such as CareerBuilder and Monster, cover all kinds of jobs.

- ✔ **Speciality (or *niche*) job boards** cover a specific group of jobs, according to factors like industry.

Job boards are established hunting grounds for vertical job search engines. You can, of course, skip the verticals if you prefer and go straight to a job board. Many people do.

The most comprehensive, searchable listing of job boards is published online by AIRS, a respected training and technology company that helps recruiters round up candidates.

Revised annually, the listing is called *AIRS Job Board and Recruiting Technology Directory*. It is available free for downloading to anyone, says AIRS chief executive officer Chris Forman. The total number of job boards listed is in the thousands, and the directory has about 100 pages. Each year's edition appears at the end of the previous year.

This valuable resource includes job sites for virtually every niche and is organised in a 'yellow pages' style: employment hubs, industry, business function, government, financial services, health care, technical, university and alumni, and contractors, both part-time and hourly. `www.airsdirectory.co.uk`.

The Continuing Power of Newspapers

The dead tree industry is done for and all the job ads are online.

We've seen and heard versions of that requiem for classified print ads in newspapers and in specialised publications during the past dozen years or so. The truth is, it's not true.

Job ads certainly are tending to go online, especially with readers under 35. There's no debate about that. And our guess is that online recruiting usage will break even with print or slightly overtake it within the next couple of years.

But here's the rest of the story

The latest reliable study says that newspaper job ads are still licking the new digital kids on the block.

It is reported that, despite the proliferation of online job boards, *three out of four jobseekers still use newspapers to look for jobs*.

The Internet was not far behind, with *three out of five jobseekers using the Net.*

More than 75 per cent in the highest group reported using the Internet in their job search, while roughly 70 per cent used newspapers. Those with household incomes below £15,000 were more likely to search newspapers (80 per cent) rather than the Internet (50 per cent).

The result? Jobseekers find work both sides of the media market.

A new wind is blowing on newspapers

Most help-wanted sections have found second homes online, so that you can search for jobs either in the touch-and-feel comfort of the pages of your own familiar newspaper or on your favourite newspaper's website. Moreover, employers who advertise with print ads often request that you send your CV online to them.

Job finding has become too complex and too challenging for you to ignore either medium. As we explain in Chapter 1, you're hunting in a New Era.

Search success is based not on where you find a job opening but on whether your responding CV sparks an interview, and what happens during that interview.

Hunting on Company Websites

No one has hard numbers on the number of company (also called corporate) websites today; suffice it to say there are so many you can't possibly look at all of them for your job hunt.

Critics accuse many corporate websites of being dated. Old school. Flat. Dull. So what? Does having the latest and greatest matter when you're hopping on a company website to see whether it offers a job you want? One viewpoint: A company with a modern website is likely to offer other innovations as well, such as new equipment and state-of-the-art training.

Another viewpoint: It makes little difference whether a company site looks and functions like a relic; the big question is: Does it offer the kinds of job you want?

Whichever viewpoint you adopt, here are things to bear in mind about submitting your CV through a corporate website.

- ✔ **Searching various company websites takes a lot of time.** Unlike general job sites, such as Monster.com and Career Builder, the universe of company websites is decentralised. Unless you're using a vertical job search engine, exploring that universe is time-consuming. You can easily spend two hours taking the measure of just a couple of corporate career sites, picking up details you need to know to maximise opportunity.

- ✔ **Research the background of a company you're truly interested in.** As you scan a company site, go back up to the home page and click to press releases, annual report, and general areas for any edge you can use to enhance your application when you move to the careers area.

- ✔ **Remember to check a potential employer's financial wellbeing.** In addition to visiting the employer's website to see what the company does, also check the company out on Yahoo Finance, and in the *Financial Times* (www.ft.com), and so forth to discover the latest news about the employer's industry. Don't be the last person employed before redundancies begin.

- ✔ **Showcase your qualifications that best match the job.** When you reach the careers area and begin submitting your CV in earnest, remember to pay close attention to each requirement of the position and customise your CV to show that your qualifications are a bull's eye for those requirements.

- ✔ **Pay attention to specific instructions on each company's site.** And don't be surprised if you're asked to take online pre-employment tests or respond to screening questions.

Some corporate sites won't accept anonymous candidates who cloak their identity. Some candidates use anonymous CVs to maintain their privacy and stay out of trouble with their current employer. An anonymous CV is stripped of the CV subject's name and contact information. Former employers may not be identified by name but described generically

(ABC Tools becomes Mid-Sized Tool Company, for instance). Anonymous CVs are distributed by job sites or third-party employment services but employers often consider them to be too much trouble to bother with.

Seeking and Finding Is Easier than Ever

As you launch your job-finding campaign, we recommend that you start with vertical job search engines as a destination for your targeted CVs; if you don't seem to be scoring winners, add general and niche job boards, as well as company websites.

As modern tools assist your job hunt, be glad that you can find job leads today much faster than ever before. But while the web is indisputably the engine driving change in the job market, career coach Mark James puts its value for most people in perspective:

> *A recipe for unemployment: Click and send, cross your fingers, and hope the phone rings.*

> *A recipe for employment: Press a full-bore campaign that includes human networking and researching job leads from all media.*

Chapter 3

Spotlighting Your CV in a Web 2.0 World

· ·

In This Chapter

▶ Discovering tech-driven ways to meet your future boss

▶ Flying in on the magic coat tails of employees and others

▶ Using online social networking services to get noticed

▶ Blogging your way to a job by reading or writing

▶ Being aware of the dark side of Internet empowerment

· ·

*W*eb 2.0 technologies – the new matchmakers in the job market – are adding opportunities for you to connect with employers. (We explain Web 2.0 and its forerunner, Web 1.0, in Chapter 1.) You can use a variety of Web 2.0 technologies, such as online social networking, blogging, RSS feeds and podcasts, to make yourself stand out from the crowd of jobseekers.

This chapter is intended to inform you, not to serve as a short-lived directory of Web 2.0 services. Instead, these pages are designed to start you off well by pointing you in newer directions.

Making Something Happen with Web 2.0 Sites

Web 2.0 sites are online services you visit to make something happen, usually with other people. The new wave of start-up hubs typically depends not on traditional top-down communication from the site's management but on bottom-up data flow from you and me and, well, everyone who wants to contribute content. Techies refer to the new services by the geeky phrase 'user-contributed content'.

You probably recognise the names of some recently popular everyone-is-smarter-than-anyone ventures. From the youth-attracting hangout at MySpace, to the video-sharing site YouTube, to the grass-roots online encyclopaedia Wikipedia, they all encourage interconnection and input. Come on in; the cyber-water's fine, they say. The services provide the technology, and the rest of us provide the substance.

These Web 2.0 services are finding their way into the job world. Many are free, drawing an income stream from ads; others charge fees. You can check out ways to use your CV to get interviews on any of them. The only way to understand this newfangled stuff is to use it. With a little practice, it's easy.

Whether you're a jobseeker with a streak of ambition a mile wide or a person who just wants to go with the flow but keep an escape hatch handy if your job starts to sink, now's the time to bone up on the rudiments of how technology can serve you in the job market.

Web 2.0 is a work in progress

The web services described in this chapter are those that are first out of the gate, but others are standing by, not yet fit enough to make it to the winner's enclosure.

To give one example of advances that, at time of writing, are not quite ready for prime time, 'mobile job search' is a promising technology under development. Imagine seeing a text message of 'Job match! We have a job for you' as you check your mobile phone while out shopping, watching your son play football or even walking along by the side of the Thames. Mobile job search technology can deliver job search result summaries to mobile phones and other hand-held devices. But for now, the technology doesn't allow candidates to apply for a position with a hand-held device. Instead, candidates must use email to respond to a job alert or to send a new CV. Those challenges will be worked out, probably in the near future.

Technology is always evolving. Stay tuned, and make it work for you.

Technology at the leading edge changes rapidly. Some observers estimate the average life span for much current technology is about 24 months. Whatever the time frame of change, its warp speed renders many details in a book quickly obsolete. Not only does technology move forward, but companies using it come and go.

Getting Involved in Online Social Networking

How do you feel about posting your persona on an e-billboard for virtually anyone to see? (Yes, social networking services insist that passwords and other privacy guards are in place, but they're far from foolproof.)

Jobseekers and employers worldwide are beginning to take a page from youth-oriented MySpace (www.myspace.com), Facebook (www.facebook.com) and other social nets as they turn to business-oriented services where people post career profiles and recruiters search for prospective employees. Consider using Twitter (http://twitter.com), a free social networking and micro-blogging service that enables users to send and read other users' updates.

What it is

Online networking services offer you help in three ways:

- Enabling you to locate contacts, who, working inside a company you'd like to be part of, are a potential source of referrals, names of managers, tips on company culture, hiring policy, and other useful information. You may have to hop from one person's profile to another to another and so forth until you reach your objective.

- Helping find managers in a company to whom you can send your CV (after breaking the ice with an exchange of email; a CV sent out of the blue is likely to be considered spam mail and deleted).

- Introducing you to recruiters who can see your profile in a virtual networking service and contact you.

Some sites are free of charge; others charge fees for contacting other members and for certain other services. A few are fee only.

Indiscreet postings on a social network can mean really big trouble for jobseekers. Many employers review profiles on social networking sites when considering candidates for jobs. Surprisingly, the young and the wireless often fail to learn from experience that it's best not to flout photos from drunken parties, stories of sexual escapades, profanity-laced comments, and similar projections of less-than-businesslike behaviour.

Professionals old enough to know better can make unintended strategy errors too. A woman called in sick so that she could join friends on a boating trip. The woman's job was on the line when her boss, checking entries on his teenage daughter's vertical network, stumbled across a dated photo of his employee enjoying white-water fun on the very day she was supposedly ill. Big oops.

The safest bet is to assume future employers will read everything you post, including extreme political or religious views and rants on any controversial topic. Here's an easy guideline to stay out of job-market trouble: Treat every online profile with the respect you give a CV.

Ways to get started

Think about online networking as comfortable connectivity. Instead of dealing with faceless strangers whom you wouldn't know if you tripped over them, you deal with individuals you know now or soon will know, and whose faces you can see and identify.

The essential process with which to hook up with an online social network follows this pattern:

1. **Someone who's already in the network invites you to join.**

   You may also be able to join without an invite – most virtual networks also let users join on their own.

2. **After selecting a virtual network that appears to include your kind of people, register, create a password and fill in a career profile.**

   (For privacy and safety, do *not* include your street address in your profile.)

3. **Explore the range of other network members who have registered with the service.**

4. **Make contacts as appropriate to your job search.**

Does your online profile do more harm than good?

Employers want to hire people whose qualifications are a good fit with the job's requirements. Recruiters often try to 'source' these candidates from scratch by identifying relevant candidates through online social networks and blogs.

The bright side of online profile sourcing is that the more information in your profile and the more sites where it's posted, the more recruiters can find you and the more they can know about you to incite their interest.

The dark side of online profile sourcing is that you risk typecasting yourself if you're a person who may be considered for several different career roles (school admissions officer, health plan co-ordinator, computer sales representative, and so on.) Pigeonholing yourself limits the range of your opportunities.

In another scenario, employers are willing to spend time checking you out online only if they're already very interested because of a referral, successful interview, or well-done CV.

A problem with some profiles is the tendency to share insider stuff that seems okay when you're speaking to friends but may not be perceived favourably by potential employers. One jobseeker wrote that she rides a motorcycle with her husband, which could raise questions about risk taking and insurance costs. Her revelation would have been positive had she been applying for a job marketing Harley-Davidsons or as a stunt double, but, alas, she wanted to be a court reporter.

The litmus test for revealing personal data in an online profile is the same as that for a CV: *Does including this information enhance my perceived qualifications for the type of job I seek?* If not, out it goes! Image is everything. Remember the workplace is not a confessional. Celebrate marketable abilities, skip private spice, and gag motormouth tendencies.

Writing about Jobs and Life: Blogs

Blogs are more plentiful than bubbles in champagne. Millions and millions of them effervesce around the globe – and even from outer space. In 2006, the space tourist and businesswoman Anousheh Ansari wrote of everyday life on the International Space Station, commenting in her blog that space smells like a 'burned almond cookie'.

Earlier blogs (web logs in the 1990s) were online personal journals filled with trivia and aimless reflections of a blogger's day. It's an understatement to say that times have changed – and at broadband speed.

The usefulness of blogs to jobseekers is in gathering attention and, some say, momentum, helped along by the morphing of those early personal journals into sleek websites that showcase content posted by one or several authors, and which welcome comments on these posts from visitors. A small but growing number of employment-related blogs are capturing audience and advertising to become media stars and influences in the job market.

What it is

You can write blogs today that show your expertise in any career field.

Company blogs aren't quite as common as grass but plenty of them are up and running. At Microsoft, for instance, employees write blogs about topics pertinent to their work; now Microsoft is using those blogs to develop a dialogue with potential employees.

Ways to get started

Finding blogs that you want to read regularly takes a bit of shopping around. Try this suggestion to kick off your hunt:

✔ **Find the right blogs for you.** One option is to use your browser. Enter a topic and add 'blog' to the search term. For example, 'employment blog' brings up a zillion possibilities.

Don't forget to look for blogs in your career field. For instance, searching for 'nurse blog' results in a long list of nursing blogs.

You can also turn to a blog search engine for blogs, such as Search4Blogs (`www.search4blogs.com`).

✔ **Time-manage your chosen blogs by reading from a free news aggregator, such as Bloglines (`www.bloglines. com`).** Once you've registered and selected the blogs you want to track, you can quickly monitor what's been posted since you last read them because new information appears in bold face. If you're tracking only one or two blogs, you can skip the news aggregator.

To establish your own blog, find a host site that offers free service for beginning bloggers – such as Blogger (`www.blogger. com`), BlogEasy (`www.blogeasy.com`), or Typepad (`www. typepad.com`) – and start writing.

Receiving Live Feeds through Really Simple Syndication (RSS)

The evolution of technology that is designed to give you a heads-up when a job you want becomes available is a bit like the difference between periodic television network news programming and 24-hour news channels. Instead of having to watch the news at 6 p.m. or 11 p.m., you can watch late-breaking news according to your timetable, whenever you want.

Familiar free recruitment agencies periodically send you email alerts about jobs that meet your specific search criteria. But the modern and also free Really Simple Syndication (RSS) technology whisks *live feeds* to your computer or hand-held devices around the clock with the latest jobs from thousands of employers and job sites.

What it is

RSS is a rapidly growing platform for the immediate distribution of online content, in this case job postings.

How does RSS beat the older email job agents? Three ways: efficiency, relevance and timeliness.

Here's how RSS works:

- ✔ Sending RSS job feeds to your RSS reader prevents email job alerts from clogging your inbox.

- ✔ RSS feeds are said to more closely target your stated requirements. Like an advanced search, you get a closer match to what you want. For example, if you're an accountant and you want a job in Milton Keynes, an email search agent may return everything with the term 'accountant' or its variations – such as accounting for lost cars in Milton Keynes. RSS job feeds are programmed to mirror your wishes.

  RSS job feeds are a wonderful way to get the first word when a new job is posted. And the feeds can be programmed to also include breaking news in industry concerns, information that could put you at the front of the queue in job interviews.

Ways to get started

How do you read RSS feeds? You can receive RSS feeds in a few different ways. You can download a news-reader program, many of which are free; use your web browser to search for 'free news-reader program'. Alternatively, some browsers and websites offer similar news-reader ability already built in. And if you're really unsure, again use your web browser to search for 'install an RSS reader'.

Chapter 4

Familiar Search Tools That Aren't Quite Dormant

* *

In This Chapter

▶ Revisiting scannable CVs

▶ Comparing plain text with eye-catching CVs

▶ Foiling identity theft and coping with spam filters

▶ Understanding online screening techniques

* *

*N*ot all web technology tools have held up under the rigours of time and progress. Certain familiar, day-to-day job search tools – job boards and company websites, for instance – retain star status in determining where to send your CVs. (See Chapter 2 for a discussion of job boards and company websites.) The eye-catching and fully formatted word-processed CV is another earlier tool that remains on the jobseekers' hit parade. The eye-catching CV reappeared about five years ago as an improvement to the drab plain text (ASCII) CV that was in vogue during the 1990s when it was the only form that older computer-scanning technology could electronically read. But other search tools from the 1990s – such as scannable and plain text CVs – are showing their age.

In this chapter, we examine the current state of selected first-born electronic technology tools used in the job market – and give you the lowdown on how they can shape your employment chances.

Scannable CVs: Same as Ever

A *scannable CV* is one that a recipient, usually an assistant in an employment office, scans into a computer as an image.

Because computers read CVs differently from how people do, you have to follow certain inconvenient rules, which we describe in this section, to be fairly sure that your scannable CV will be read as you intended.

A scannable CV may start life as a paper document that you can post, hand deliver, or fax using a fax machine; the employer uses a scanning machine to enter a hard copy CV into a candidate database. More often these days, you create a scannable CV on your computer and email it to an employer, who electronically enters it directly into a database.

When an employer has your scannable CV, computer software extracts from it a summary of basic information, pulling out factors like your name, contact information, skills, work history, years of experience, and education. Scanned CVs and their extracted summaries sleep peacefully until an HR specialist or recruiter searches the summaries by keywords to retrieve candidates who match the requirements of a job opening. The technology ranks candidates from the most qualified to the least qualified. The relevant CVs get a wake-up call and pop to the recruiting screen, where human eyes take over the recruiting tasks.

Stop and ask directions

Although scannable and plain text CVs are heading the way of carbon paper, and the vast majority of readers prefer to cast their eyes over the eye-catching CV, you need to make a reality check. You're job hunting in a time of transitioning technology, including an explosion of filters that will not accept Word attachments. The attachments are refused as a way to avoid viruses and to keep out spam (including CV spam).

This means that you can never be 100 per cent sure what technology is being used where you want to send your CV. The solution is to ask, by telephone or by email, the company's human resources department or the company's receptionist the following question:

I want to be sure I'm using your preferred technology to submit my CV. Can I send it as an attachment, say in MS Word?

Alternatively, if you don't have a clue, you can send your CV within the body of your email as plain text and also attach it as a word-processed document.

The old/new fax trick

Sometimes you may find it advantageous to go back to basics when your online CVs never seem to result in a call back. If you can get the name and fax number of the human resources manager for a job you want, try sending the manager your scannable CV by fax.

Sending scannable CVs by post is another option, especially effective with older, conservative managers and company owners. Traditional employers in some professions, such as Law and Accounting, may prefer to read CVs drafted on traditional paper.

The once-desirable scannable CVs are on their way out, joining MS DOS (operating software) in computer museums. Recruiters now prefer the newer intake systems that allow CVs to travel smoothly online and move straight into an electronic CV-management database without the need to conform to scanning rules.

Even so, don't trash your scannable CV just yet. If an employer or job site directs you to send a CV that can be scanned, do it. And do it well, so that your CV doesn't go AWOL in a database. Take the following steps to prevent scanning errors from putting you on the sidelines:

✔ **Use type that's clear and readable.** Don't use a condensed typeface. White space separates letters; no space jumbles them together. Letters must be distinctively clear with crisp, unbroken edges. Avoid arty, decorative typefaces. Typefaces such as Times Roman, Verdana, Arial and Helvetica are very easy to read.

✔ **Avoid these bad-scan elements:**

- Italics or script

- Underlining

- Reverse printing (white letters on a black field)

- Shadows or shading

- Hollow bullets (they read like the letter o)

- Hash signs (#) for bullets (the computer may read it as a phone number)

- Boxes (computers try to read them like letters)

- Two-column formats or designs that look like newspapers

- Symbols, such as a logo

- Vertical lines (computers read them like the letter *l*)

- Vertical dates (use horizontal dates: 2006–2010)

✔ **Feel free to use larger fonts for section headings and your name.** A font size of 14 to 16 points is good. Larger headings look better on the electronic image of your CV when humans read it (which they don't always do). We recommend you format the body of your CV in a 12-point font size, the section headings in 14-point, and the name in 16-point.

✔ **Do keep your scannable CV simple in design and straightforward.** Recruiters like it because it doesn't confuse computers.

✔ **Do send your paper CV without staples.** Paper clips are okay. Follow this tip for all CVs that you post or hand deliver because staples are a pain to pull out before feeding into a scanner one page at a time.

Plain Text CVs: A Long Last Gasp

The plain text CV (also known as an ASCII CV) is an online document constructed without formatting in plain text file format. It is most often sent by email, but can be sent by fax, post or courier.

The main characteristic about this CV is its looks (or lack of same). It's so ugly, only a computer could love it. See Figure 4-1 for an example of a plain text CV.

```
MARY BLOGGS
38 ANGLE TOWN
Tel: 000 0000 0000
Mobile: 00000 000 000
Email: marybloggs@yahoo.com

KEY SKILLS

Sound experience in financial/general administration in diverse settings
Ability to work on own initiative under pressure and to tight deadlines
Excellent interpersonal and negotiating skills for forging external
relations
Practical knowledge of Microsoft Series and associated software
Adapt well to challenges; resourceful and innovative

PROFESSIONAL/CAREER

2003-2007     (Name of company)
              Administrator
              Undertook comprehensive management of small company,
              implementing quality assurance standards and ensuring
              efficiency at all times. Carried out financial control,
              processing payment transactions and related data,
              preparing VAT details and contributing to annual accounts.
              Issued information as to internal procedures,
              disseminating information and maintaining general company
              records. Created business and marketing strategies.

PROFESSIONAL/QUALIFICATIONS

1996-1999     University of Greenwich
              Bachelor of Science (Hons), Computing Science

1994-1996     Lewisham College
              BTEC National Diploma in Computer Studies

1993-1994     Lewisham College
              First Diploma in Business Finance

1991-1993     Hatcham Wood School
              Six GCSE subjects

Also completed course in Microsoft Excel 5.4

PERSONAL INFORMATION

Interests: Family life; walking; reading

REFERENCES AVAILABLE UPON REQUEST
```

Figure 4-1: Plain Text (ASCII) CV.

Converting your CV to plain text (ASCII)

Although plain text CVs are heading into the sunset, until the recruiting world is totally living large with formatted e-CVs, you may be stuck with the plain-Jane look. So here's the drill. Create your CV in MS Word, go to File, then Save As, and choose Plain text (.txt) in the Save as type option, which converts it to plain text (ASCII).

If that doesn't work, try the following:

1. **Highlight your CV by clicking Edit → Select All.**

2. **Copy your CV by clicking Edit → Copy.**

3. **Open Notepad (or TextEdit on a Mac).**

   To get there click Start → Programs → Accessories → Notepad. (Simply click on the icon in the Dock (or in Applications) on a Mac.)

4. **Click Edit → Paste to paste your CV into Notepad.**

5. **Turn on the 'Word-wrap' feature by choosing Format → Word-Wrap.** (Or Wrap to Page in TextEdit.)

6. **Save the CV.**

   Make sure you name it with your name so that potential employers can easily find it – for example, JohnGill.txt.

   Because your CV now has ASCII for brains, it won't recognise the formatting commands that your word-processing program uses.

When you send your ASCII CV, paste it with a covering note (a very brief letter) into the body of your email.

Avoiding ASCII landmines

Keep the following points in mind as you create a CV that you may want to convert later to an ASCII file:

- Don't forget to spell-check *before* you save your CV as an ASCII file.

- Don't use any characters that aren't on your keyboard, such as 'smart quotes' (those tasteful, curly quotation marks that you see in this book) or mathematical symbols. They don't convert correctly, and your CV will need fumigating to rid itself of squiggles and capital 'U's.

> You know that you're off in the wrong direction if you have to change the Preferences setting in your word processor or otherwise go to a lot of trouble to get a certain character to print. Remember that you can use dashes and asterisks (they're on the keyboard), but you can't use bullets (they're *not* on the keyboard).

Although you can't use bullets, bold or underlined text in a plain text document, you can use plus signs (+) at the beginning of lines to draw attention to part of your document. You can also use a series of dashes to separate sections and capital letters to substitute for bold face. When you don't know what else to use to sharpen your ASCII effort, you can always turn to Old Reliable – white space.

Be on guard against other common ASCII landmines:

- **Typeface/fonts:** You can't control the typeface or font size in your ASCII CV. The text appears in the typeface and size that the recipient's computer is set for. This means that bold face, italics, or different font sizes don't appear in the online plain text version. Use all caps for words that need special emphasis.

- **Word wrap:** Don't use the word wrap feature when writing your CV because it will look as weird as a serial letter *E* running vertically down a page. Odd-looking word wrapping is one of the cardinal sins of online CVs. Set your margins at 0 and 65. Then end each line after 65 characters with hard carriage returns (press the Enter key) to insert line breaks.

- **Proportional typefaces:** Don't use proportional typefaces that have different widths for different characters (such as Times Roman). Instead, use a fixed-width typeface (such as Courier) so that you have a true 65-character line. For example, if you compose and send your CV in Courier 12 and it's received in the Arial typeface, it should still work well with most email programs, surviving transport with a close resemblance to the original line length.

- **Tabs:** Don't use tabs; they get wiped out in the conversion to ASCII. Use your space bar instead.

- **Alignment:** Your ASCII CV is automatically left-justified. If you need to indent a line or centre a heading, use the space bar.

E-Forms: Filling in the Blankety-Blanks

The e-form is just a shorter version of the plain text CV, and you usually find it on company websites. The company encourages you to apply by entering your plain text into designated fields of the forms on the site.

The e-form is almost like an application form, except that it lacks the legal document status an application form acquires when you sign it, certifying that all facts are true. Sometimes the e-form has a stipulation saying that by completing and returning the form, you're stating that the facts are true. Other employers make it clear that if short-listed, you'll have to sign the form at the interview to confirm the information is true.

Follow the on-screen instructions given by each employer to cut and paste the requested information into the site's template. You're basically just filling in the blanks with your contact information that's supplemented by data lifted from your plain text CV.

Remember that e-forms can't spell-check, so cutting and pasting your CV into the e-form body, instead of typing it in manually, is your best bet. Because you spell-checked your CV before converting it to ASCII (of course, you did!), at least you know that everything is likely to be spelled correctly.

Virtually all company websites now encourage you to apply online through their applicant portals. You're asked to fill out an online form, upload, or cut and paste your CV. Most companies ask you to answer demographic questions about race, gender and so forth. You aren't required to include this information to be considered for employment. Nevertheless, women and minorities are well advised to oblige the demographics request. What if you're a white male? Your call.

The subject line online

Whether you're sending a scannable, plain text, or eye-catching word-processed CV online, the subject line of your email can bring you to the forefront of a recruiter's attention.

✔ When you respond to an advertised job, use the job title. If none is listed, use the reference number.

✔ When you send a CV, write a short 'sales' headline. For example: Bilingual teacher, soc studies/6 yrs' exp. Or, Programmer, experienced, top skills: Java, C++.

Never just say *Bilingual teacher* or *Programmer*. Sell yourself! Keep rewriting until you've crammed in as many sales points as possible.

Do you need to show a 'cc' for 'copy sent' on your CV? If you're emailing a recruitment manager (such as the accounting manager), copy the human resources department manager; that saves the hiring manager from having to forward your CV to human resources and is more likely to result in your landing in the company's database to be considered for any number of jobs.

The Fully Designed, Eye-Catching CV Is Back!

Before electronic and online CVs came along, the good-looking paper CV was the gold standard. The best sported a number of compelling embellishments: attractive formatting, appealing typefaces and fonts, bold-faced headings, italics, bullets and underlining. The embellishments, tastefully done, were refreshing to read until technology all but killed them off more than a decade ago in favour of the electronically correct but truly dull plain text CVs we describe in the section 'Plain Text CVs: A Long Last Gasp'.

The eye-catching CV was wonderful and was sorely missed by CV readers who grew bleary-eyed looking at pure text the whole day long.

Attachment etiquette

Here are a few pitfalls CV senders need to avoid when emailing attachments:

✔ **Do not attach EXE files.** An Executable file could contain a virus, and no one will chance having the hard drive or network infected.

✔ **Do not attach ZIP files.** Who's to say the ZIP file doesn't contain an infected Executable. And besides, can your CV be so large that you have to ZIP it?

✔ **Do not attach password-protected documents.** How would you expect someone or something to open it without the password?

That's in the past. Smart technology has brought back the good-lookers we gave up in the '90s to make sure our CVs arrived intact over the Internet. Now you can usually attach your CV as a fully formatted, handsome dog of a document in a word-processing program, usually MS Word.

From Identity Theft to Recruiter Turn-Off: Why CV Blasting Is a Bad Idea

CV blasting services (also jokingly known as CV spamming services) advertise their willingness to save you time and trouble by 'blasting' your CV to thousands of recruiters and recruitment managers all over the Internet – for a fee, of course. The pitches are tempting, but should you avail yourself of this miraculous service? Just say no! CV blasting can bring you big trouble, from making identity theft easier for crooks, to irritating your boss, to making you an 'untouchable' for recruiters.

Privacy and identity theft problems

Concerning identity theft issues, privacy expert Pam Dixon advises being cautious with your CV's information. On her non-profit World Privacy Forum (www.worldprivacyforum. org), she continually updates a must-read report titled 'Job Seeker's Guide to CV: Twelve CV Posting Truths'.

Truth Number One says this: 'If you're going to post a CV online, post your CV privately. Most job sites offer anonymous posting that lets you mask your contact information and email address when you post a CV. This posting option allows you to decide who sees your real information, such as your home address. Masking this information is perhaps the single most important step jobseekers who want to post a CV online can take to protect themselves.'

Get your CV past spam gatekeepers

You may not know whether your CV becomes cyber-litter because a spam or virus filter deletes it unread. Here are some tips for getting your CV where you want it to go:

✔ Do send email to only one company at a time. If your ISP (Internet Service Provider) suspects you're sending out a battalion of messages, its computers may kill your work. On the receiving end, filters may see a large number of addressees as incoming spam and eliminate your CV.

✔ Do look at the junk mail you get and avoid using subject lines with exclamation points, all capitals, or spam buzzwords, such as 'free,' 'trial,' 'cash,' or 'great offer.' Even appropriate phrases like 'increased sales to 10,000 pounds a month,' can trigger spam filters, thanks to junk pitches such as 'Make 10,000 pounds a month from home working part time.' When you're in doubt, try spelling out pound amounts.

✔ Don't use too many numbers in your email address, such as jobseeker12635@yahoo. com. Filter software may think the numbers are a spammer's tracking code.

✔ Send your CV to yourself and see whether it lands in your junk filter bin. One software expert runs every CV and covering note through three spam filters on his computer before emailing them.

Is Pam Dixon overreacting? No. The media has been full of horror stories of identity theft for some years.

Admittedly, merely being careful about releasing your CV information online won't keep you safe from identity theft in these days when the guard rails on privacy are coming down in so many ways in so many places. But do be stingy with your private information.

Identity theft may be the worst-case scenario, but it isn't the only life-altering problem that can arise when you put your business on e-street.

Overexposure to recruiters

One more reason not to spread your CV all over the map: When you're targeting the fast track to the best jobs, nothing beats being brought to an employer's notice by an important third person – and an independent recruiter qualifies as an important third person.

Employers are becoming resistant to paying independent recruiters big fees to search the web when they theoretically can save money by hiring in-house corporate recruiters to do it. That's why recruiting agencies need fresh candidates that employers can't find elsewhere. If you want a third-party recruiter to represent you, think carefully before pinning cyber-wings on your CV.

In addition to losing control of your CV, its wide availability can cause squabbles among contingency recruiters over who should be paid for finding you. An employer caught in the conflict of receiving a CV from multiple sources, including internal databases, will often pass over a potential employee rather than become involved in deciding which source, if any, should be paid.

Online Screening Keeps On Keepin' On

Online screening is an automated process of creating a blueprint of known requirements for a given job and then collecting information from each applicant in a standardised manner to see whether the applicant matches the blueprint. The outcomes are sent to recruiters and hiring managers.

Online screening is known by various terms – *prescreening* and *pre-employment screening,* to mention two. By any name, the purpose of online screening is to verify that you are, in fact, a good fit for the position and that you haven't lied about your background. Employers use online screening tools (tests, assessment instruments, questionnaires, and so forth) to reduce and sort applicants against criteria and competencies that are important to their organisations.

If you apply online through major job sites or many company website career portals, you may be asked to respond 'yes' or 'no' to job-related questions, such as:

- ✔ Do you have the required degree?

- ✔ Do you have experience with (specific job requirement)?

- ✔ Are you willing to relocate?

- ✔ Do you have two or more years' experience managing a corporate communications department?

- ✔ Is your salary requirement between £55,000 and £60,000 a year?

Answering 'no' to any of these kinds of questions disqualifies you for the listed position, an automated decision that helps the recruiters thin the herd of CVs more quickly but that could be a distinct disadvantage to you, the jobseeker. (Without human interaction, you may not have enough of the stated qualifications, but you may have compensatory qualifications that a machine won't allow you to communicate.)

On the other hand, professionals in shortage categories, such as nursing, will benefit by a quick response. Example: *Are you a Grade E Nurse?* If the answer is 'yes,' the immediate response, according to a recruiter's joke, is 'When can you start?'

Sample components of online screening

The following examples of online screening aren't exhaustive, but they are illustrations of the most commonly encountered upfront filtering techniques.

✔ **Basic evaluation:** The system automatically evaluates the match between a CV's content (jobseeker's qualifications) and a job's requirement and ranks the most qualified CVs at the top.

✔ **Skills and knowledge testing:** The system uses tests that require applicants to prove their knowledge and skills in a specific area of expertise. Online skills and knowledge testing is especially prevalent in information technology jobs where dealing with given computer programs is basic to job performance. Like the old-time typing tests in an HR office, there's nothing subjective about this type of quiz: You know the answers, or you don't.

✔ **Personality assessment:** Attempts to measure work-related personality traits to predict job success are one of the more controversial types of online testing. Dr Wendell Williams, a leading testing expert, says that personality tests expressly designed for hiring are in a totally different league from tests designed to measure things like communication style or personality type: 'Job-related personality testing is highly job-specific and tends to change with both task and job,' he says. 'If you are taking a generic personality test, a good rule is to either pick answers that fall in the middle of the scale or ones you think best fit the job description. This is not deception. Employers rarely conduct studies of personality test scores versus job performance and so it really does not make much difference.'

✔ **Behavioural assessment:** The system asks questions aimed at uncovering your past experience in applying core competencies the organisation requires (such as fostering teamwork, managing change) and position-specific competencies (such as persuasion for sales, attention to detail for accountants). We further describe competencies in Chapter 6.

✔ **Managerial assessments:** The system presents applicants with typical managerial scenarios and asks them to react. Proponents say that managerial assessments are effective for predicting performance on competencies, such as interpersonal skills, business acumen and decision making. Dr Williams identifies the many forms these assessments can take:

  • **In-tray exercises**, where the applicant is given an in-tray full of problems and told to solve them.

- **Analysis case studies**, where the applicant is asked to read a problem and recommend a solution.

- **Planning case studies**, where the applicant is asked to read about a problem and recommend a step-by-step solution.

- **Interaction simulations**, where the applicant is asked to work out a problem with a skilled role player.

- **Presentation exercises**, where the applicant is asked to prepare, deliver and defend a presentation.

- **Integrity tests**, which measure your honesty with a series of questions. You can probably spot the best answers without too much trouble.

Pros and cons of online screening

Here's a snapshot of the advantages and disadvantages of online screening, from the jobseeker's perspective:

- **Advantages:** In theory, a perfect online screening is totally job-based and fair to all people with equal skills. Your CV would survive the first screening, which assesses only your ability to do well in the job. You are also screened out of consideration for any job you may not be able to do, saving yourself stress and keeping your track record free of false starts.

- **Disadvantages:** The creation of an online process is vulnerable to human misjudgement; we're still looking for an example of the perfect online screening system. Moreover, you have no chance to 'make up' missing competencies or skills. (An analogy: You can read music, but you don't know how to play a specific song. You can learn it quickly, but there's no space to write 'quick learner'.)

Can your CV be turned away?

What if you get low grades on answering the screening questions – can the employer's system tell you to take your CV and get lost? No, not legally. Anyone can leave a CV, but if they don't pass the screening, the CV will be ranked at the bottom of the list in the database.

Level playing field for salaries

If employers demand your salary requirements before they grant you an interview, you're at a disadvantage in negotiating strength. You can get an idea as to how much you're worth by scanning the advertisements, online or in the newspapers, of similar positions that you're applying for.

Hundreds of websites also broadcast compensation information supplied by `www.reed.co.uk`, `http://career-advice.monster.com` and `www.celreconsultancy.co.uk`. With a few clicks, get a free ballpark estimate of your market worth.

The bottom line is that if you don't score well in screening questions, your CV will be exiled to an electronic no-hire zone even if it isn't physically turned away.

Match Your CVs to the Jobs

Part I covers new Web 2.0 and surviving Web 1.0 online job search tools. Knowing both the latest and the traditional methods is critical to move your CVs along cyberways and byways that lead to interview offers.

But never forget that to get past software filters, your CVs must spell out your qualifications for the jobs' requirements. If you're parking your CVs in an online database rather than responding to a specific job ad, make sure they specify that you possess the most commonly requested requirements in a given career field.

Part II
The Rise and Reign of the Targeted CV

'A very impressive CV, Brother Dominic.'

In this part . . .

You find special tips and targeted CV guidance to use to show off your strengths and shine the best light on your not-so-strengths. You also get tips for CVs when you want to change your career field or occupation. We also explain how to give your content the zing it needs to make sure it's a looker.

Chapter 5

Creating Your Best CV

· ·

In This Chapter

▶ Selling your value to people you want to work for

▶ Focusing your CV like a high-powered laser

▶ Selecting the format that champions your image

▶ Comparing format features in case you're not sure

· ·

*H*ow much are you worth to employers? Your CV inspires their first best guess, so you want to make sure it's a compelling portrait of your strengths and skills. Paint yourself in murky colours on a stained canvas, and you're likely never to get in the door. This chapter shows you how to structure your CV so that you come off as a masterpiece.

'Telling It' Mutes; 'Selling It' Sings

Pretend you're in the market for replacement windows in your home. Which of the following two messages would better tweak your interest in taking a closer look at the company?

The Turner Group has been in existence replacing windows for 30+ years at the same easy-to-find showroom. We offer 25 different models and window sizes – a choice to fit every home and budget.

The Turner Group has been assisting homeowners to protect their home values with 25 models of high-quality replacement windows at discount prices – and in all sizes – since the mid-1970s.

The first statement is an example of telling it; the message is 'look at us!' The second statement is an example of selling it, and its message is 'Here's what we can do for you.'

Targeted CVs don't tell it – they sell it! Dry, dull descriptions of what you did on a job are as boring as videos of a friend's childhood birthday parties.

Instil excitement! List your background facts but make sure you position them as end-user (employer) benefits.

One way to sell your value and your benefits to an employer who has the power to hire you is to get specific. Communicate the importance of what you've done by using details – numbers, names, achievements, outcomes, volume of sales or savings, and size of contracts, for example.

Remember, when you sell it, you breathe life into a rigid, dreary, boring and generally coma-inducing document. Table 5-1 provides several examples of the sell-it strategy for CVs.

Table 5-1	Selling Your CV
Tell It	**Sell It**
Supervisor of HR generalist and recruiting functions for 10 years at company headquarters.	Supervisor with 10 years' successful management of 6 HR generalists and 3 recruiters for regional company with 3 administrative offices and 8 manufacturing plants.
Worked as network administrator with responsibility for administration and troubleshooting.	As network administrator, created in excess of 750 user scripts, installed 16 workstations, administered security codes to 350 clients, supervised installation of company-wide Microsoft XP Pro, and regularly solved stress-causing malfunctions in operating system and software.
Leading sales rep for new homes in prestigious development in year when housing market began to cool.	In a cooling housing market (down 11% from previous year), became No.1 sales rep, selling £7,800,000 in 12 months – 13 homes at £600,000 each.

Other chapters of this book clue you in on more techniques of approaching your CV with a sell-it mindset, the starting gate of today's high-stakes CV derby. In the classic film *Butch Cassidy and the Sundance Kid,* Butch Cassidy tells Sundance: 'You have vision but the rest of the world wears bifocals.' Help employers see not only what you were responsible for but how well you did it and why it mattered.

Focusing Your CV

Too many jobs in your background threaten your focus. *Unfocused* is an ugly word in job-search circles, one that indicates you lack commitment, that you're perpetually at a fork in the road. Lack of focus is a reason *not* to employ you.

 When your CV looks as though it will collapse under the weight of a mishmash of jobs unconnected to your present target, eliminate your previous trivial pursuits. Group the consequential jobs under a heading that says *Relevant Work Experience Summary.*

What if this approach solves one problem – the busy CV – but creates another, such as a huge, gaping black hole where you removed inconsequential jobs? Create a second work history section that covers those holes, labelling it *Other Experience.* Figure 5-1 shows an example.

Dealing with an unfocused career pattern on paper is easier when it's done under the banner of a temp job agency. The treatment in this case lists the temp job agency as the employer. You choose one job title that covers most of your assignments. Under that umbrella title, identify specific assignments. Give the dates in years next to the temp job agency, skipping dates for each assignment. Figure 5-2 shows an example.

Impacted CV with Focus

Professional Experience

UNITECH, Hamburg, Germany
Computer Laboratory Assistant, [dates]
        Manage and troubleshoot hardware and software systems. Recover data, create programming architecture, and install parts and software. Assist a team of 18 engineers.

TECHNIK TECH, Hamburg, Germany
Assistant to System Analysts, [dates]
        Participated in construction, repair, and installation of systems at local businesses. Diagnosed faulty systems and reported to senior analysts, decreasing their workload by 25%.

TRADE NET, Berlin, Germany
Applications and Network Specialist, [dates]
        Set up and monitored a Windows-based BBS, including installation, structure, security, and graphics. Authored installation scripts for Trade Net, licensing U.S. software use in Europe.

Other Experience

AMERICAN TOY STORE, Berlin, Germany, Sales Representative, [dates]
Arranged and inventoried merchandise, directed sales and customer relations. Developed strong interpersonal skills and gained knowledge of retail industry.

CAMP INTERNATIONAL, Oslo, Germany, Activities Director, [dates]
Organized daily activities for more than 300 children from English-speaking countries, including sports, recreation, and day classes. Supervised 10 counselors and kitchen staff of five, developing responsible and effective management skills.

Figure 5-1: Solving the black-hole problem in a jobs-impacted CV by creating a focus plus a second work history section.

What if you work for several temp agencies at the same time? The simple answer is that you use the same technique of dating your work history for the temp agencies, not for the individual assignments. This dating technique is a statement of fact; you legally are an employee of the temp job agency, not of the company that pays for your temporary services.

Focusing with Temp Jobs

Professional Experience

Relia-Temps   [dates]

Executive Secretary

- North Western Banking Group
Perform all clerical and administrative responsibilities for 10-partner investment and loan firm, assisting each partner in drafting contracts, reviewing proposals, and desiging various financial programs. Supervise 7 staff members. Introduced 50% more efficient filing system, reducing client reviews from 4 to 3 hours.

Administrative Assistant

- Mosaic Advertising
Supervised 3 receptionists and 4 clerical specialists, reporting directly to president. Administered daily operations of all accounting and communication transactions. Using extensive computer savvy, upgraded company computer networks withWindows 98.

- Blakeslee Environmental, Inc.
Assisted 8 attorneys at interstate environmental protection agency, scheduling meetings and conferences, maintaining files, and updating database records. Redesigned office procedures and methods of communication, superior organizational skills.

Figure 5-2: Listing your temporary job assignments without looking unfocused.

When excess jobs or focus isn't a problem, you may choose an alternative presentation for a series of short-term jobs. The alternative doesn't mention the staffing firm(s) but only the names of the companies where you worked.

CV Formats Make a Difference

CV format refers not to the design or look of your CV but to how you organise and emphasise your information. Different format styles flatter different histories.

Thinking out of the CV box

CVs aren't limited to paper. You can actually create electronic CVs. Although you probably won't need to go to that extreme – and, in fact, many employers prefer that you don't, you may want to know the pros and cons of each.

✔ **Video CVs:** A *video CV* (or *video podcast*) is actually a canned video interview in which a candidate speaks about his qualifications, goals and strengths. Employers shy away from video CVs because they fear a candidate's image and sound could lead to discrimination charges being brought against them by old, minority, fat or ugly candidates.

✔ **Web CVs:** *Web CVs* (or *e-portfolio* or *HTML CVs*) are electronic documents that you post on a personal website. The format may simply display credentials, or it may go glamorous with links to sound and graphics from your work samples. Jobseekers in cutting-edge technology fields, theatre, marketing and design are attracted to this form of presentation.

✔ **Multimedia CVs:** *Multimedia CVs* are similar to web CVs, but they're on a disk that can be sent by post. An attention-getting novelty in the 1990s, they're rarely used today.

At root, formats come in two main types:

✔ The standard format lists all employment and education, beginning with the most recent and working backwards.

✔ The targeted CV shouts what you can do instead of relaying what you've done and where you did it.

✔ The executive format shows what you've achieved from what you did.

The following sections explore each type of CV format so that you can choose the style that is best for you and your skills.

The standard (reverse chronological) format

The standard (reverse chronological) format, shown in Figure 5-3, is straightforward: It cites your jobs from the most recent backwards, showing dates as well as employers and educational institutions (college, vocational-technical schools, and career-oriented programmes and courses). You accent a steady work history with a clear pattern of upward or lateral mobility.

<u>**Diana Larkins**</u>
63 Shakespeare Road,
Stratford-On-Avon
Tel: 00000 000 000

EMPLOYMENT HISTORY

2007-Date	**Mother Hubbard Nursery**
	<u>Nursery Nurse</u>
	Attend to toddlers, devising numerous leisure-orientated activities to raise levels of achievement in basic reading and writing. Implement strict health/safety policies, liaising extensively with parents regarding children's progress and well-being. Participate in drafting daily programmes.
2006-2007	**Sun Allied Group**
	<u>Stock Room Assistant</u>
	Coordinated daily workload within a demanding environment, ensuring efficiency and accuracy at all times. Carried out stock devolution, price control and replenishment. Utilised customised software to perform tasks.
2002	**Dorothy Perkins; Burtons**
	<u>Sales Assistant</u>
	High volume of public liaison, issuing information/advice as to appropriate merchandise and resolving general queries. Processed payment transactions and reconciled money on a daily basis. Other duties included price and stock control.

PROFESSIONAL/QUALIFICATIONS

NVQ 2 in Childcare (Greenwich College)
NVQ 2 in Business Administration (Crossways College)
'A' Level Health and Social Care, Four GCSE subjects (Blackheath Bluecoat School)

PERSONAL INFORMATION
Date of Birth: January 1, 1987
Interests: Socialising, fashion, music

REFERENCES AVAILABLE UPON REQUEST

Figure 5-3: The tried-and-tested, standard, reverse chronological format.

Strengths and weaknesses

Check to see whether the standard reverse chronological CV's strengths are yours:

- ✔ This upfront format is by far the most popular with employers and recruiters because it is so, well, upfront.

- ✔ The standard format links employment dates, underscoring continuity. The weight of your experience confirms that you're a specialist in a specific career field (social service or technology, for example).

- ✔ The standard format positions you for the next upward career step.

- ✔ As the most traditional of formats, the standard format fits traditional industries (such as banking, education and accounting).

Taking the weaknesses of the standard, reverse chronological format into account:

- ✔ When your previous job titles are substantially different from your target position, this format doesn't support your objective. Without careful management, the standard format reveals everything, including inconsequential jobs and negative factors.

- ✔ The standard format can spotlight periods of unemployment or brief job tenure.

- ✔ Without careful management, it reveals your age.

- ✔ Without careful management, it may suggest that you were stuck in a job for too long.

Who can use this format and who needs to think twice

Use the standard reverse chronological format if you fall into any of these categories:

- ✔ You have a steady school and work record reflecting constant growth or lateral movement.

- ✔ Your most recent employer is a respected name in the industry, and the name may ease your entry into a new position.

✔ Your most recent job titles are impressive stepping stones.

✔ You're a savvy writer who knows how to manage potential negative factors, such as inconsequential jobs, too few jobs, too many temporary jobs, too many years at the same job, or too many years of age.

Think twice about using the standard format under these circumstances:

✔ You have a lean employment history. Listing a stray student job or two is not persuasive, even when you open with superb educational credentials enhanced with internships and work experience.

✔ With careful attention, you can do a credible job by extracting from your extracurricular activities every shred of skills, which you present as abilities to do work with extraordinary commitment and a head for quick learning.

✔ You have work-history or employability problems – gaps, demotions, stagnation in a single position, job hopping (four jobs in three years, for example), re-entering the workforce after a break to raise a family.

Exercise very careful management to truthfully modify stark realities. However, you may find that other formats can serve you better.

Creating a standard (reverse chronological) CV

To create a standard CV, remember to:

✔ Focus on areas of specific relevance to your target position.

✔ List all pertinent places you've worked, including for each the name of the employer and the city in which you worked, the years you were there, your title, your responsibilities and your measurable achievements.

To handle problems such as unrelated experience, you can group unrelated jobs in a second work history section under a heading of Other Experience, Previous Experience or Related Experience. We tell you more about handling special circumstances in Chapter 9.

The targeted format

The targeted format, shown in Figure 5-4, is a CV focusing on your skills and experience for the particular position you want. It ignores chronological or reverse chronological orders and concentrates on getting relevant skills or experience on the front page to grab attention straightaway. It elaborates on information that is relevant, and downplays that which is not so competitive. Contemporary targeted CVs list employers, job titles and dates. Job descriptions are very important, because this is where the transferable skills come into play if you're testing the waters and changing your career, or if you want to elevate yourself to that glass window in Canary Wharf.

Strengths and weaknesses

The following are the strengths of the targeted format:

✔ A targeted CV directs a reader's eyes to what you want him to notice. It helps a reader visualise what you can do instead of when and where you learned to do it. Targeted CVs salute the future rather than embalm the past.

✔ The targeted format – written after researching the target company – serves up the precise functions or skills that the employer wants. It's like saying, 'You want budget control and turnaround skills – I have budget control and turn-around skills.' The skills sell is a magnet to reader eyes!

✔ It uses unpaid and non-work experience to your best advantage.

✔ It allows you to eliminate or subordinate work history that doesn't support your current objective.

Weaknesses of the targeted format include the following:

✔ Because recruiters and employers are more accustomed to standard reverse chronological formats, departing from the norm may raise suspicion that you're not the cream of the crop of applicants. Readers may assume that you're trying to hide inadequate experience, educational deficits, or who knows what.

✔ Targeted styles may leave unclear which skills grew from which jobs or experiences.

✔ This style doesn't make a clear career path obvious.

MARK PARSONS
0000000 0000000, Tel: 0000 0000
Email: 000000

Experienced in research management and associated remits in diverse settings
Practical knowledge of Microsoft Series, Adobe Photoshop and related Internet tools

PROFESSIONAL/QUALIFICATIONS

2006 – Date	**University of Life Long Learning** Bachelor of Arts (Hons 2:1) - Modern and Medieval History
1998 – 2005	**The Cremean School** GCSE A'Level subjects: Art (A); Mathematics with Statistics (B); Late Modern History (A); English Language and Literature (B) 10 GCSE subjects (Grades A- C)

RELEVANT EMPLOYMENT SUMMARY

2009	**The Archives and Local Studies** Archivist (Voluntary) Collate documents from archives, digitising data to be accessed by researchers. Extensive liaison with both corporate and private clients. Maintain public records.
2008	**The Chancery Lane Inn** Archive Research Officer Collaborated with solicitors to conduct research on Right of Way issues. Identified and secured sources for information such as maps and records. Interpreted data and compiled findings.

OTHER EMPLOYMENT SUMMARY

2006 – 2008	**Silver Services** General Assistant Summer appointments in hospitality at V.I.P. marquees.
2005 – 2006	**Platinum Gold Sports** General Assistant Controlled crowds at Foxes and Hounds Club football matches.

Interests:
Keen writer, art, world politics, current affairs, reading
Date of Birth: September 10, 1987

REFERENCES AVAILABLE UPON REQUEST

Figure 5-4: Focusing on skills and experience relevant to the position.

Who can use this format and who needs to think twice

This CV is heaven-sent for career changers, new graduates, ex-military personnel, seasoned aces, and individuals with multitrack job histories, work-history gaps or special-issue problems.

Jobseekers with blue-ribbon backgrounds and managers and professionals who are often tapped by executive recruiters need to avoid this format.

Creating a targeted CV

Choose areas of expertise acquired during the course of your career, including education and unpaid activities. These areas become skill and functional headings, which vary according to the target position or career field. Note any achievements below each heading. A few examples of headings are: *Management, Sales, Budget Control, Cost Cutting, Project Implementation* and *Turnaround Successes.*

List the headings in the order of importance and follow each heading with a series of short statements of your skills (refer to Figure 5-4). Turn your statements into power hitters with measurable achievements.

Executive format

An executive format is slightly long-winded (say, three to five pages) but factual. It emphasises professional qualifications, activities and, most importantly, key achievements and skill. This format is shown in Figure 5-5.

Be aware that executive CVs are reviewed under a microscope and every deficiency stands out. Adding a portfolio that shows your experience-based work skills may compensate for missing chunks of formal requirements. Just make sure that any unsolicited samples you send are high quality and need no explanation.

Who can use this format and who needs to think twice

Professionals in senior management, IT, marketing or any other industry that needs the candidate to elaborate on his professional and personal achievements at previous jobs can use this CV. For example, a senior sales manager for a telecommunications company may allude to the fact that he exceeded sales targets for one particular year, or orchestrated a multi-million pound launch project in Europe. Or, an IT project manager may mention achievements in setting up and rolling out a series of networks across UK and European branches.

Figure 5-5: The effective executive format is perfect for certain careers.

The content shown in the figure:

PERCY DESIGNER
6 Carpenters Road, Surrey, 000 000
Tel: 00000 000 000; 00000 0000 0000
E-mail: woodandnails@yahoo.com

KEY SKILLS

- Solid experience in design architecture and associated roles in diverse global settings
- Sound ability to initiate/execute major design projects to achieve significant results
- Ability to recruit/orchestrate interdisciplinary multi-national and indigenous teams
- First-rate analytical skills to assimilate data and create solutions
- Excellent interpersonal and negotiating skills to forge partnerships
- In-depth knowledge of AutoCAD, proficiency in 2D, 3D
- Fluent in English and Arabic

KEY ACHIEVEMENTS

- Honours graduate in Architectural Engineering
- Spearheaded refurbishment of mansion for Saudi sheikh
- Collaborated with Aviary private residence for Qatar Royal Family
- Senior management of multi-million pound refurbishment projects
- Instrumental in expansion to global markets such as USA and Egypt

PROFESSIONAL/CAREER

Dec 2006–Date   **The Bird Cage**
(Interior, Operations and Procurement)
Senior Manager
Assigned to influential sheikh from Saudi Arabia as
Client Representative. Undertook comprehensive management of
extensive refurbishment/remodeling of mansion on the River
Thames in Berkshire.

Also executed major refurbishment to other properties belonging
to sheikh's family's private estate. Prepared feasibility studies
and design proposals for 15-million pound investment fund by
sheikh in London.

Key projects:
Private dwellings in Grosvenor Square, Palace Gate, Belgrave
and Mayfair, ranging to £500,000.

Continue with your career history in reverse chronological order, then your qualifications.

Also use it when common-sense convention makes it the logical choice, as when you're applying for a top-level civil service appointment.

Creating an executive CV

Follow the template in Figure 5-5, paying attention to accomplishments. Just because you present yourself in a low-key, authoritative manner doesn't mean that you can forget to say how good you are.

Academic curriculum vitae

The academic CV is a comprehensive biographical statement, typically three to ten pages, emphasising professional qualifications and activities. A CV of six to eight pages, ten at the most, is recommended for a veteran professional; two to four pages is appropriate for a young professional just starting out.

If your CV is more than four pages long, show mercy and save eyesight by attaching an *executive summary* page to the top. An executive summary gives a brief overview of your qualifications and experience.

Strengths and weaknesses

A CV presents all of the best of you, which is good, but for people with ageing eyes, a CV may be too reading-intensive. More important, weaknesses in any area of your professional credentials are relatively easy to spot.

Who can use this format and who needs to think twice

Anyone working in a PhD-driven environment, such as higher education, think tanks, science, and elite research and development groups needs to use this format.

Everyone else, avoid using it if you can.

Creating an academic curriculum vitae

Create a comprehensive summary of your professional employment and accomplishments: education, positions, affiliations, honours, memberships, credentials, dissertation title, fields in which comprehensive examinations were passed, full citations of publications and presentations, awards, discoveries, inventions, patents, seminar leadership, foreign languages, courses taught – whatever is valued in your field.

CONSTANCE ZEPHANIAH
The Green Room, Thornton Heath
Manchester, 00 00

SPECIALIST DISCIPLINES

Strategic Management
Knowledge & Information Management
Organisation Analysis, Electronic Commerce

PROFESSIONAL/QUALIFICATIONS

1980–2000	**University of Hammersmith**
(2000)	Ph.D in Management
(1991)	M. Phil. in Information Systems
(1987)	Postgraduate Diploma in Business Analysis
1983	**University of London**
	Higher Diploma in Business Studies

PROFESSIONAL/CAREER

Sept 2006–Date	**School of Business**
	Associate Professor
Nov 1993–Aug 2007	**City University of London**
	(Faculty of Business)
(June 2002–Aug 2007)	Assistant Professor
(Nov 1993–June 2000)	Lecturer

KEY ACHIEVEMENTS

(Tertiary):
Finalist for the Teaching Excellence Award of City University of London;
Consistently rated as one of the best teachers in universities at which employed

Excellent teaching evident from impeccable results of student evaluation;
Superior teaching team management skills.

(Administration/Professional Services):
Appointed to key committees for quality assurance in teaching/person development;
Forged solid links with the business, industry and professional sectors;

(Educational Research):
Recipient of Earmarked Research Grant Award;
Funded for diverse projects, including refereed publications in international journals;
Published more than 30 articles, including key journal papers

PROFESSIONAL/RELATED

2005–Date	**Simmons School**
(2007–Date)	Task Force Member
	Integral to review and
	implementation of programme
	Validation/accreditation.

Figure 5-6: Brevity definitely isn't a feature of the academic CV.

(2006–Date)	Committee Representative Initiate/implement change process for education, research and services to the community. Review various academic issues.
2001–2006	**City University of London** Applied Research Co-ordinator High volume of liaison with corporate and industry agencies, forging effective working relations.
2003	**City University of London** Departmental Co-ordinator (Business Practice Internship) Secured internship for 17 Year Two students with companies.
1994–2001	**City University** (BBA/IS Programme) Committee Member/Year One Tutor Facilitated tutorials for students on course Development and professional/personal development.

ADDITIONAL:

2005–Date

Blake University
Republic of the Philippines and Hong Kong Management Association
External Assessor for PhD Dissertation in Business Administration

2000–Date
Review papers for international journals and conferences, including *Information Systems Journal, Electronic Markets, South African Computer Journal, Electronic Journal on Information Systems in Developing Countries*, Americas Conference on Information Systems, Pacific Asia Conference on Information Systems

2002
University of South Asia (2003)
External Examiner for a PhD thesis entitled: 'Extending the action research approach as an operational method for the maintenance of a management information system: An exploratory field study in China'.

Blake University
Certification course on 'Object-Oriented Analysis and Design using UML'

RESEARCH PROJECTS

To Date
Investigator of (CERG) project – 'Information Requirements Determination and IT Application for Caseworkers'

Chief Invigilator of research project
'The Application of Web 2.0 Technologies Grant award'

Figure 5-6 *(continued)*

2002–2006
E-learning project supported and funded by the City & Lilburn.
Development of hybrid model and course cartridge for online delivery of
fundamental MIS courses to undergraduate students. Total funding:
£14,000.

1990–1997
PhD research on application of soft systems methods and object-
oriented analysis for determining organisational information
requirements. The primary contribution of this research lies in bringing
together the competencies and strengths of multiple methodologies.

Figure 5-6 *(continued)*

Making Contact with a Speculative Letter

When you're doing a targeted mailing campaign, a speculative letter attracts attention because it reads more like a story than a document. The speculative letter is a combination of covering letter and CV; often it is one page. It typically opens with a variation of the question: 'Are you looking for a professional who can leap high buildings in a single bound?' A speculative letter opening may look something like this:

> *Should you be in the market for an accomplished, congenial senior human resources specialist who has earned an excellent reputation for successful HR technology acquisition analysis and management, this letter will be of interest to you.*

The letter continues to give a basic overview of a jobseeker's strengths, including previous employers, achievements, skills and competencies, as they would apply to the recipient company.

Even though you use the post to send a speculative letter, take care to discover the key qualifications most often required for the position you seek. Targeting is a no-lose strategy even for cold mailings.

Your strengths message may be in paragraph form or in bulleted statements. The speculative letter format can be especially useful for a professional with an abundance of experience. But don't substitute a speculative letter when you're responding to a job advertisement that asks for a CV. The employer calls the shots.

One of the most amazing placements we've ever heard about was the case of the chemist who at age 50 left the profession to have a go dealing cards at a casino. Five years later, at age 55, he wanted to return to the chemistry workplace. A cold mailing of a well-written CV letter to owners of small chemical companies earned a caretaker CEO job while the owner took an extended two-year trip out of the country.

Highlighting Your Best Work with a Portfolio

Samples of your work, gathered in a portfolio, have long been valuable to fields such as design, graphics, photography, architecture, advertising, public relations, marketing, education and contracting.

Often, you deliver your portfolio as part of the job interview. Some highly motivated jobseekers include a brief version of a career portfolio when sending their CVs, although recruiters say that they want fewer, not more, CV parts to deal with.

If you must include work samples to back up your claims, send only a few of your very best.

The portfolio is a showcase for documenting a far more complete picture of what you offer employers than is possible with a CV of one or two pages. Getting recruiters to read it is the problem. When you determine that a portfolio is your best bet, take it to job interviews. Put your portfolio in a three-ring binder with a table of contents and tabs separating its various parts. Mix and match the following categories:

- ✔ **Career goals** (if you're a new graduate or career changer): A brief statement of less than one page is plenty.

- ✔ **Your CV:** Use a fully formatted version in MS Word.

- ✔ **Samples of your work:** Include easily understandable examples of problem solving and competencies.

- ✔ **Proof of performance:** Insert awards, honours, testimonials and letters of commendation, and flattering performance reviews. Don't forget to add praise from employers, people who reported to you, and customers.

- ✔ **Proof of recognition:** Here's where you attach certifications, transcripts, degrees, licences and printed material listing you as the leader of seminars and workshops. Omit those that you merely attended unless the attendance proves something.

✔ **Military connections:** The Territorial Army provides exceptionally good training, and many employers know it. List military records, awards and badges.

 Make at least two copies of your portfolio in case potential employers decide to hold on to your samples or fail to return them.

Make sure your portfolio documents only the skills that you want to apply within a job. Begin by identifying those skills, and then determine which materials prove your claims of competency.

Choosing the Approach That Works for You

The big closing question to ask yourself when you've settled on a format is:

Does this format maximise my qualifications for the job I want?

If the format you've chosen doesn't promote your top qualifications, take another look at the choices in this chapter to select a format that helps you paint a sparkling self-portrait.

Chapter 6

Flowing Content Versus Jarring Detail

● ●

In This Chapter

▶ The sections of your CV

▶ Grabbing attention with a skills summary

▶ Opting for a summary

▶ Including competencies on your CV

● ●

*Y*ou're confident that you have the right attitude and skills for the position, and surely the prospective employer will take a chance on you. But getting past the recruitment stage is a hurdle you need to clear. You may know that you're perfect for the job, but now you need to convince the recruitment manager. Your CV contents are the first steps to reaching the finishing line before others. In other words, what your CV says is mission-critical.

Exploring the Sections of Your CV

Chapter 5 speaks of selling, not telling, your worth. Citing your earned accomplishments and achievements are how you make that happen. To capture the best job, you know that you can't simply add the latest job description and recalculate the same old CV with updated data.

Focus on your best content and present it forcefully. Because you have very few words to work with, choose precisely the correct words; Chapter 7 takes you to the word desk. Don't rush the construction of your CV: If you build it right, the interviews will come.

The best CVs include the following core sections:

- ✔ Contact details
- ✔ Key skills
- ✔ Experience
- ✔ Education and training
- ✔ Honours and awards
- ✔ (Optional) Hobbies and other interests

Putting your Career Objective on a CV is outdated and not at all effective in today's high-tech CV formatting. Your Career Objective is normally implied if you've graduated with a Bachelor of Science degree in Ophthalmology or you completed a course in Social Work two months ago. If you target your CV well in the first place, you do not have to remind the prospective employer that you want to climb the corporate ladder. If you're changing careers, the key skills, described in the section 'Hooking the Reader with Your Key Skills,' later in this chapter, will announce your intention if properly written.

No more than you want to carry around a couple of stones of extra weight do you want fat in your CV – family, early education, favourite things and so on. Trim it! The rule for including information on your CV is simple: *If the data doesn't support your objective to be invited for an interview, leave it out.*

Leading with Contact Details

If the employer thinks you're a perfect match for the job, then she needs to be able to find your contact information right away. Don't bury this critical information in your CV. Always start the CV with your contact details. For some senior managers and executives, such as relations managers in Information Technology, the contact details are left for the last page of the CV. A senior executive may start the CV with a Key Skills box, or a synopsis of career highlights.

Your contact details need to include the following:

✔ **Name:** No matter which format you choose, place your name first on your CV. If your name isn't first, a job computer may mistake Excellent Sales Representative for your name and file you away as Ms Representative. You may want to display your name in slightly larger type than the rest of the contact information, and in bold face.

✔ **Address:** Some people cite personal privacy and identity theft as reasons you should not include your address on the CV. However, there may be what is called an *applicant tracking system*, also called a candidate management system or applicant management system. By any name, an ATS is a software application designed to help a company recruit employees more efficiently. At minimum, an ATS usually includes features to post job openings online, screen CVs, acknowledge receipt of CVs, and generate interview requests by email to potential employees.

ATS systems check your email address and sometimes your physical address to look for duplicates. If you leave off your physical address, the system may not accept your CV, or if it does, you may not receive an acknowledgment if the company sends acknowledgment communications by post.

Unless you have a reason to hide your physical location, which you can do with a PO box address, continue to give a street name, town/city and postcode.

If you're a university student or member of the military who'll be returning home, give both addresses, labelled *Current Address* and *Permanent Address.* You can add operational dates for each address, but don't forget to delete a date after it's passed. Otherwise, you may lose out on interviews if the prospective employer replies to you by post.

✔ **Valid telephone number:** Use a personal phone number, including the area code, where you can be reached or where the recruiter can leave a message.

If you must share a telephone with kids, emphasise the need for them to answer the phone professionally and to keep their calls short. In addition to – or instead of – a landline, give your mobile telephone number.

Is it okay to list your work telephone number on your CV? In a decade when employers have been tossing workers out without remorse, it's a tough world and you need speedy communications. The practical answer is to list your work number if you have a direct line and voicemail, or a mobile phone.

✔ **Other contact media:** Also give your email address, and, if you have one, your web page address.

What about using company resources? Should you ever use your employer's email address or letterhead? Many employers see an employee's use of company resources to find another job as small-time theft.

In certain situations, however, you can use your company's help. For example, when a company is downsizing, it's expected to provide resource support for outplacement. Contract employment is another exception: When you're ending the project for which you were employed, your employer may encourage you to use company resources.

Including a Hook: Your Key Skills

Your CV needs a hook to grab attention within three seconds. You can do this by summarising your Key Skills that are relevant to the position. Insert this section just below your contact details. Automatically, the prospective employer will look at this section and the more powerful the skills listed, the more likely you are to be short-listed!

Avoid long-winded narratives about how enthusiastic, reliable and flexible you are. Really, you're expected to be all of this, and employers are tired of reading such words, especially 'dynamic'. It's definitely 1980s and will make the employer scream silently in mental anguish.

Compile your skills in a Key Skills, Skills Profile or Core Skills (any of these titles are fine) section. This section comprises four to seven sentences across the page and reflects on all the skills you'll bring to the position.

For example, say that you see an advertisement for a photographer, and you have experience in both film and digital processes. You can use the first sentence to highlight this:

'Extensive background in film and digital photography across all genres'. Or, you're a teacher seeking a position in primary education. You can say: 'More than 10 years' experience in primary/secondary education'. In this instance, although the ad demands someone with primary education skills, you're immediately showing the prospective employer that you have more than that.

Here are examples of skills you can use for your Key Skills section:

- ✔ Solid experience in financial management in diverse fields
- ✔ Sound knowledge of SAGE Line 150 and associated tools
- ✔ Ability to work under pressure to challenging deadlines
- ✔ Excellent negotiating skills to forge partnerships
- ✔ Fluent in English, French and basic Spanish
- ✔ Adapt well to challenges, resilient and tenacious
- ✔ More than 10 years' experience in oil and gas engineering
- ✔ Solid knowledge of global risk and health/safety rules
- ✔ Ability to orchestrate multi-tasked teams and achieve results
- ✔ Excellent interpersonal skills and ability to deliver training

Note: Professional skills are usually written towards the top of the list. Try to keep each sentence short, sweet and staccato, as the saying goes. The last thing an employer wants to see is a block of text waffling on about how wonderful you are as a worker and person, such as, 'An extensive career in IT; I am well-versed in all software/hardware engineering.' Repetitive and, with an extensive background, it is implied you would have experience in most software and hardware anyway!

The beauty about writing a Key Skills section is that you can change the contents to suit the purpose of the CV. If you're a photographer with great skills, you say so. On the other hand, if you decided two years ago that photography was not fulfilling anymore, and you ventured into the North Sea to become a trainee rig worker, then you change the Key Skills box to mention your experience at sea first.

Making Education and Experience Work for You

Without a doubt, the two most important elements of your CV are employment and education. They carry equal weight when applying for most jobs, although in certain industries experience has more emphasis than education. For example, as a support worker in a semi-independent care profession, you might have ten years' experience in dealing with challenging behaviour, an NVQ Level Three in Advice and Guidance, but no degree. Here, your experience far outweighs qualifications.

Education

When providing information about your education, list your highest degree first: type of degree, university name and date awarded. Follow these tips:

- New graduates need to give far more detail on course work than graduates who've held at least one post-graduation job for one year or more.
- Omit secondary school or primary school if you have a college degree.
- If you have a vocational-technical school certificate or diploma that required less than a year to obtain, list your secondary school as well.
- Note continuing education, including seminars related to your work.
- If you fall short of the mark on the job's educational requirements, try to compensate by expanding the continuing education section. Give the list a name, such as *Professional Development Highlights,* and list every impressive course, seminar, workshop and conference that you've attended.

Experience

List all your experience within the last ten years in reverse chronological order. Include specific job titles, company names and locations, and dates of employment. Show progression and promotions within an organisation, especially if you've been with one employer for eons.

What's first, education or experience?

Not sure whether to list your education or experience at the top of the CV? The general rule in CV writing is to lead with your most qualifying factor.

With certain exceptions (such as law, medicine and accountancy) that may require more rigorous licensing than other professions, lead off with experience when you've been in the workforce for at least one year. When you're loaded with experience but low on credentials, list your school days at the end.

Including Competencies

Most good CVs focus on knowledge, skills and accomplishments. They only hint at competencies required to do the work. Competencies are based on your personal strengths to fulfil the demands of the job, such as presence of mind, working under pressure or being able to complete major projects. Competencies are more often demonstrated on application forms than in the more succinct CV format. To capture behavioural competencies on a CV, you must show how your accomplishments confirm your competencies. Or to turn it around, you must show how your competencies made it possible for you to achieve goals.

Not sure what to include? The accomplishments that most interest employers include:

- ✔ Increased revenue
- ✔ Saved money
- ✔ Increased efficiency
- ✔ Cut overheads
- ✔ Increased sales
- ✔ Improved workplace safety
- ✔ Purchasing accomplishments
- ✔ New products/new lines
- ✔ Improved record-keeping process

> ✔ Increased productivity
>
> ✔ Successful advertising campaign
>
> ✔ Effective budgeting

To connect your behaviours with your accomplishments, you can say:

> **Product development:** *Created new mid-market segment supporting an annual growth rate of 20 per cent in a flat industry, demonstrating high energy and business acumen.*

In the above example, the verb 'demonstrating' connects the accomplishment (Created new mid-market segment supporting an annual growth rate of 20 per cent in a flat industry) with competencies (high energy and business acumen).

Other verbs you can use to bridge the two types of information include:

> ✔ Confirming
>
> ✔ Displaying
>
> ✔ Exhibiting
>
> ✔ Illustrating
>
> ✔ Manifesting
>
> ✔ Proving
>
> ✔ Revealing
>
> ✔ Verifying

Gaining Extra Points

You've covered the meat and potatoes of your CV content. What can you add that will strengthen your image? You can, for instance, draw from your activities to show that you've got the right stuff. John Gill applies for a position as field worker with an international non-government organisation (NGO). He paid his own expenses to spend his university Easter break building houses for the poor in Romania. That act of sacrifice shows Gill's character, that he has gained insight into multi-culturalism and can relate to persons from diverse economic backgrounds. In this example, that's good CV content.

What's in your diary and how will it strengthen your image? Here are a few thoughts on the nitty-gritty of buffing your image.

Activities

Activities can be anything from hobbies and sports to campus extracurricular participation. The trick is to analyse how each activity is relevant to the target job; to discuss skills, knowledge or other competencies developed; and to list all achievements.

Make sure that this section doesn't become meaningless filler, however. In addition, avoid potentially controversial activities: Stating that you love fox hunting won't endear you to animal-loving recruiters.

If you've been able to research the person reading and have found that you two have a common interest, list it on your CV so that it can become an icebreaker topic during an interview. Or, if you're a voluntary worker at a summer play scheme applying for a position of a teacher's assistant, this is relevant.

Organisations

Give yourself even more credentials with professional and civic affiliations. Mention all important offices held. Relate these affiliations to the person reading your CV in terms of marketable skills, knowledge and achievements.

A high profile in the community is particularly important for sales jobs.

Just as you need to be careful about which activities you identify (see preceding section), you also need to be sensitive to booby traps in organisation memberships:

⮡ Listing too many organisations may make the reader wonder when you'd have time to do the job.

✔ Noting that you belong to one minority group organisation may work in your favour, but reporting your membership of five minority group organisations may raise red flags. The recruiter may worry that you're a troublemaking activist.

✔ And, of course, you know better than to list your membership of religious or political organisations (unless you're applying for a job that requires such membership). They don't apply to your ability to do the job, and some people reading your CV may use them to keep you out of the running.

Honours and awards

List most of the achievements for which you were recognised. If the achievement had nothing to do with work or doesn't show you in a professional light, don't take up white space with it; for example, you probably wouldn't list a Chilli Cook-Off award unless you're applying for a job as a chef. Awards may include being the regional Salesperson of the Year or winning a scholarship to university. Or perhaps being selected to represent the company at an international event or being a gold medallist for ikebana floral arrangement. Well, the last one only if you're applying for interior decorating positions.

Licences and work samples

If you're in the legal, certified accounting, engineering or medical profession, add to your CV the appropriate licence, certifications and other identifications required for the position.

For a professional CV, you may also list descriptions or titles of specific work that you've done, or include samples of your work along with your CV. If asked to include samples of your work, be selective about what you send. These samples are usually attached to the CV. Unlike a portfolio that shows projects or assignments for architects, artists or models, sample material is simply elaboration of the projects you've already alluded to on the CV. The reason for adding sample work is to ensure the main body of the CV isn't laboured with too much technical or industry jargon. Separating the sample work gives you the option of submitting the section with the CV.

Shaping Your Content on Application Forms

Application forms (paper or online) aren't CV content, but they're close to it. Filling out these forms requires a shift in what you say because you have to sign them, *making the application form a legal document*. Lies can come back to bite you. Stick to the facts as you follow these rules:

- ✔ If you complete an application form online, look out for the instructions on signatures. Some forms ask you to double-click on a button to confirm you're submitting, others state that by submitting the form, you confirm that the information you give is true.

- ✔ If you're applying on hard copy, where possible, take the application home where you won't be rushed and can spend adequate time polishing your application to get it just right. Photocopy the application form before you begin in case you find errors on the original (or spill coffee on it) and need a clean copy.

- ✔ Verify all dates of employment and salaries to the letter.

- ✔ Enter the full name and last known address of former employers. If former employers are no longer available, don't substitute co-workers.

- ✔ If asked for salary history, give your base salary (or add commission and bonuses), omitting benefits.

- ✔ Give a complete employment history in months and years, including trivial three-week jobs that you wisely left off the CV. If you don't tell the whole story, you leave a loophole of withholding information that later can be used against you if the employer decides that you're excess.

- ✔ Unless you have a condition directly affecting your ability to do the job for which you're applying, you need not elaborate on any disability.

- ✔ Be honest about having collected unemployment benefits (but remember that fraudsters are frowned on); if you're caught lying about it later, practise your farewell speech.

- ✔ Autograph the application; you've been honest – why worry?

Content to Omit: Your Salary Story

Never mention salary on your CV. Full stop.

Sometimes a job ad asks for your salary history or salary requirements. Be aware that revealing pound figures in advance puts you at a disadvantage. This is especially true if you've been working for low pay – or if you've been paid above the market rate.

In addition to job ads, profile forms on job websites almost always ask for your salary information. If you decide to participate, state your expectations and include the value of all perks (benefits, bonuses), not just salary, in your salary history. But be realistic about your salary expectations by comparing the rates of salaries for similar positions (refer to Chapter 4).

When you choose to disclose your salary history or requirements online, make a distinction between general information forms and formal signed applications (legal documents). Include benefits (total compensation) on general information forms, but omit benefits on formal signed applications that ask for 'salary history'.

Chapter 7

Words That Make the Mark

. . . .

In This Chapter

▶ Selling yourself with buzz words

▶ Making your mark with keywords

▶ Following simple grammar rules

▶ Remembering to check your spelling

. . . .

*W*inston Churchill needed only two words to bind Russia to the *Iron Curtain*. And brief four words memorialised Martin Luther King's vision: *I have a dream.* Just like these famous wordsmiths, you can use captivating words to grab a choice job. But choose unwisely, and your CV won't stand out from the crowd. In this chapter, we walk you through choosing the right words to make your CV sing.

Using Words to Bring Good News

Buzz words are action verbs describing your strengths: *improve, upgrade, schedule.* *Keywords* are usually nouns demonstrating essential skills: *technology transfers, PhD organic chemistry, multinational marketing.* A smattering of both can make your CV sing from the rafters. An absence of either can make your CV mute.

No matter how much you like the word, try not to use the same one twice on your CV. The thesaurus in a word-processing program can give you more possibilities.

The last word on buzz words is that little words never devalue a big idea. Remember, when your words speak for you, you need to be sure to use words that everyone can understand and that relate to the job in hand. Value your words. Each one is a tool for your future.

Buzz words for administration and management

Administrators and managers are usually at the end of the office spectrum, but both positions are pivotal to ensuring efficient daily operations. Use these buzz words in your CV:

Advised	Initiated	Prioritised
Approved	Inspired	Processed
Authorised	Installed	Promoted
Chaired	Instituted	Recommended
Consolidated	Instructed	Redirected
Counselled	Integrated	Referred
Delegated	Launched	Reorganised
Determined	Lectured	Represented
Developed	Listened	Responded
Diagnosed	Managed	Reviewed
Directed	Mediated	Revitalised
Disseminated	Mentored	Routed
Enforced	Moderated	Sponsored
Ensured	Monitored	Streamlined
Examined	Motivated	Strengthened
Explained	Negotiated	Supervised
Governed	Originated	Taught
Guided	Oversaw	Trained
Headed	Pioneered	Trimmed
Influenced	Presided	Validated

Buzz words for maximum effect

Replacing two or three words with one word makes your CV crisper and easier to read. For example, instead of saying 'I was responsible for setting up and running a project', simply say 'I initiated a project'. Use these buzz words to be a bit more creative in your CV:

Acted	Edited	Proofread
Addressed	Enabled	Publicised
Arranged	Facilitated	Published
Assessed	Fashioned	Realised
Authored	Formulated	Reconciled
Briefed	Influenced	Recruited
Built	Initiated	Rectified
Clarified	Interpreted	Remodelled
Composed	Interviewed	Reported
Conducted	Introduced	Revitalised
Constructed	Invented	Scheduled
Corresponded	Launched	Screened
Costumed	Lectured	Shaped
Created	Modernised	Stimulated
Critiqued	Performed	Summarised
Demonstrated	Planned	Taught
Designed	Presented	Trained
Developed	Produced	Translated
Directed	Projected	Wrote

Buzz words for sales and persuasion

Negotiating is a major role in marketing, procurement, purchasing and other industries that demand interfacing with clients. The words you use on the CV need to demonstrate selling and persuasion skills. Try to fit in some of these buzz words:

Arbitrated	Judged	Purchased
Catalogued	Launched	Realised
Centralised	Lectured	Recruited
Consulted	Led	Reduced
Dissuaded	Liaised	Reported
Documented	Maintained	Repositioned
Educated	Manipulated	Researched
Established	Marketed	Resolved
Expedited	Mediated	Restored
Familiarised	Moderated	Reviewed
Identified	Negotiated	Routed
Implemented	Obtained	Saved
Improved	Ordered	Served
Increased	Performed	Set goals
Influenced	Planned	Sold
Inspired	Processed	Solved
Installed	Produced	Stimulated
Integrated	Promoted	Summarised
Interpreted	Proposed	Surveyed
Investigated	Publicised	Translated

Buzz words for technical ability

Some CVs have to include technical jargon, but using verbs to break up terminologies makes the documents easier to absorb:

Analysed	Expedited	Operated
Broadened	Fabricated	Packaged
Charted	Facilitated	Pioneered
Classified	Forecast	Prepared
Communicated	Formed	Processed
Compiled	Generated	Programmed
Computed	Improved	Published
Conceived	Increased	Reconstructed
Conducted	Inspected	Networked
Coordinated	Installed	Reduced
Designed	Instituted	Researched
Detected	Integrated	Restored
Developed	Interfaced	Revamped
Devised	Launched	Streamlined
Drafted	Lectured	Supplemented
Edited	Maintained	Surveyed
Educated	Marketed	Systematised
Eliminated	Mastered	Trained
Excelled	Modified	Upgraded
Expanded	Moulded	Wrote

Buzz words for office support

Even if you're just entering the job market and hope to land yourself a job as the office junior, you still need to write your CV in authoritative tones. Use a smattering of these buzz words in your CV:

Adhered	Distributed	Managed
Administered	Documented	Operated
Allocated	Drafted	Ordered
Applied	Enacted	Organised
Appropriated	Enlarged	Packaged
Assisted	Evaluated	Planned
Assured	Examined	Prepared
Attained	Executed	Prescribed
Awarded	Followed up	Processed
Balanced	Formalised	Provided
Budgeted	Formulated	Recorded
Built	Hired	Repaired
Charted	Identified	Reshaped
Completed	Implemented	Resolved
Contributed	Improved	Scheduled
Co-ordinated	Installed	Screened
Cut	Instituted	Searched
Defined	Justified	Secured
Determined	Liaised	Solved
Dispensed	Maintained	Started

Buzz words for teaching

Using words that illustrate your ability to plan and deliver teaching programmes is crucial to enhance your chances of being short-listed for the job, whether you're a nursery teacher or a university lecturer. Try these on for size:

Acquainted	Designed	Influenced
Adapted	Developed	Informed
Advised	Directed	Initiated
Answered	Dispensed	Innovated
Appraised	Distributed	Installed
Augmented	Educated	Instituted
Briefed	Effected	Instructed
Built	Empowered	Integrated
Certified	Enabled	Lectured
Chaired	Enacted	Listened
Charted	Enlarged	Originated
Clarified	Expanded	Persuaded
Coached	Facilitated	Presented
Collaborated	Fomented	Responded
Communicated	Formulated	Revolutionised
Conducted	Generated	Set goals
Co-ordinated	Grouped	Stimulated
Delegated	Guided	Summarised
Delivered	Harmonised	Trained
Demonstrated	Implemented	Translated

Buzz words for research and analysis

If you're a business analyst, research officer or academic, you can benefit from using specific words to show how familiar you are with relevant terminologies:

Administered	Detected	Interviewed
Amplified	Determined	Invented
Analysed	Discovered	Investigated
Applied	Documented	Located
Articulated	Drafted	Measured
Assessed	Edited	Obtained
Audited	Evaluated	Organised
Augmented	Examined	Pinpointed
Balanced	Exhibited	Planned
Calculated	Experimented	Prepared
Charted	Explored	Processed
Collected	Extracted	Proofread
Compared	Focused	Researched
Compiled	Forecast	Reviewed
Composed	Found	Riveted
Concentrated	Generated	Screened
Conducted	Grouped	Summarised
Constructed	Identified	Surveyed
Consulted	Integrated	Systematised
Critiqued	Interpreted	Unearthed

Buzz words for helping and care work

Social workers and care managers have to demonstrate their skills and abilities by using words that are indicative of the professions:

Advanced	Encouraged	Reassured
Advised	Enabled	Reclaimed
Aided	Facilitated	Rectified
Arbitrated	Familiarised	Redeemed
Assisted	Fostered	Referred
Attended	Furthered	Reformed
Augmented	Guided	Rehabilitated
Backed	Helped	Repaired
Balanced	Instilled	Represented
Boosted	Liaised	Served
Braced	Mentored	Settled
Clarified	Ministered	Supplied
Collaborated	Negotiated	Supported
Comforted	Nourished	Stabilised
Consoled	Nursed	Streamlined
Consulted	Nurtured	Translated
Contributed	Obliged	Treated
Counselled	Optimised	Tutored
Demonstrated	Promoted	Unified
Diagnosed	Provided	United

Buzz words for financial management

Finance has its own industry jargon. Selecting the right words can pronounce you as a worthy candidate:

Adjusted	Economised	Reported
Administered	Eliminated	Researched
Allocated	Exceeded	Reshaped
Analysed	Financed	Retailed
Appraised	Forecast	Returned
Audited	Funded	Saved
Balanced	Gained	Shopped
Bought	Generated	Secured
Budgeted	Increased	Sold
Calculated	Invested	Solicited
Computed	Maintained	Sourced
Conciliated	Managed	Specified
Cut	Marketed	Supplemented
Decreased	Merchandised	Systematised
Developed	Planned	Tested
Disbursed	Projected	Tripled
Dispensed	Purchased	Underwrote
Distributed	Quadrupled	Upgraded
Doubled	Reconciled	Upsized
Downsized	Reduced	Vended

Buzz words for many skills

Here's a list of buzz words you can use for all industries:

Accomplished	Evaluated	Overhauled
Achieved	Executed	Performed
Adapted	Facilitated	Prioritised
Adhered	Forecast	Promoted
Allocated	Founded	Proposed
Appraised	Governed	Reconciled
Arbitrated	Guided	Rectified
Arranged	Illustrated	Remodelled
Articulated	Improved	Repaired
Assured	Increased	Reshaped
Augmented	Initiated	Retrieved
Collected	Integrated	Solved
Communicated	Interpreted	Stimulated
Composed	Invented	Streamlined
Conceptualised	Launched	Strengthened
Conserved	Led	Trained
Contributed	Navigated	Upgraded
Co-ordinated	Optimised	Validated
Demonstrated	Organised	Won
Dispensed	Originated	Wrote

Unlocking Your Talents with Keywords

Recruiters and employers use keywords to search and retrieve e-CVs in databases for available positions. Keywords are chiefly nouns and short phrases. That's your take-home message. But once in a while, keywords can be adjectives and action verbs. Employers choose their own list of keywords, which is why no list is universal.

Avoid poison words

Recruiters advise staying away from the following words on your CV:

✔ **Responsibilities included:** Make your CV accomplishment-driven, not responsibilities-driven. Job-description language tells, not sells, in a CV.

✔ **Dismissed:** Don't let this word slip into your CV if you want it to escape being lost in a database. *Laid-off* or *reduction in force* generally aren't good terms either, but you can use them when circumstances make it sound as though you were fired. A *lay-off* or *a reduction in force* implies the action was no fault of yours, but *fired* suggests that you screwed up. The basic rule: Don't state why you left a position; save the explanation for an interview.

✔ **References available upon request:** References are assumed.

Save the space for more important information.

✔ **National Insurance Number:** Never make yourself vulnerable in this era of identity theft. Don't submit your NI Number unless specifically requested.

✔ **Assisted with, worked with, helped with:** Did you really just assist or help someone else? Were you standing by watching someone else do the work? Use action verbs to describe how you contributed to each achievement.

✔ **Also:** The word is unnecessary (for example, 'Manage budget of £1 million. *Also* interface with consultants'.) Write tightly. Eliminate *also, an, the* and *and* wherever you can. Use the saved space to pack more punch, and the CV won't lose meaning.

In computerised job searches, keywords describe not only your knowledge base and skills but also such things as well-known companies, big-name colleges and universities, degrees, licensing, and professional affiliations.

Keywords identify your experience and education in these categories:

- Skills
- Technical and professional areas of expertise
- Achievements
- Professional licences and certifications
- Other distinguishing features of your work history
- Prestigious schools or former employers

Employers identify keywords, often including industry jargon, that they think represent essential qualifications necessary for high performance in a given position. They specify those keywords when they search a CV database.

Rather than stopping with action verbs, connect your achievements. You managed *what?* You organised *what?* You developed *what?* Job computers look for the *whats,* and the whats are usually nouns.

Keywords are arbitrary and specific to the employer and each employer search. So the keywords (qualifications) in each job ad are the place to start as you customise your CV for the position. But you need to make educated guesses, not when you're responding to advertised jobs, but merely when warehousing your CV online. The following lists provide a few examples of keywords for selected career fields and industries.

Keywords are the magnets that draw eyes to your talents.

Keywords for administration/ management

Use plain English in your CV and avoid using too much in-house or industry jargon. Smatter your CV with these keywords:

Administrative processes	Facilities management
BA, BSc or similar	Front office operations
Back office operations	Office manager
Benchmarking	Operations manager
Budget administration	Policy and procedure
Change management	Production schedule
Crisis communications	Project planning
Data analysis	Records management
Document management	Regulatory reporting

Keywords for banking

Professionals in the banking sector undertake many diverse roles at any one time. Using appropriate keywords shows multitasking and avoids repetition:

Branch manager	Loan management
Branch operations	Loan recovery
Commercial banking	Portfolio management
Construction loans	Retail lending
Credit guidelines	ROE (Return on Equity)
Debt financing	ROI (Return on Investment)
FILO (First In, Last Out)	Trust services
Financial management	Turnaround management
Investment management	Uniform commercial code filing
Investor relations	Workout

Keywords for customer service

Whether you're a sales assistant in a High Street outlet, a receptionist at a doctor's surgery or a manager of an engineering company, you conduct customer relations. Using these keywords sets you ahead of the pack:

Account representative	Help desk
Call centre	Key account manager
Customer communications	Order fulfilment
Customer focus groups	Order processing
Customer loyalty	Product response clerk
Customer needs assessment	Records management
Customer retention	Sales administration
Customer retention innovations	Sales support administrator
Customer service manager	Service quality
Customer surveys	Telemarketing operations
Field service operation	Telemarketing representative

Keywords for information technology

IT, like finance and medicine, uses a high volume of technical jargon. Avoid using long sentences to describe processes you undertake. Use these useful keywords:

Automated voice response (AVR)	Global systems support
Chief information officer	Help desk
Client/server architecture	Multimedia technology
Cross-functional team	Network development analyst
Data centre manager	Project lifecycle
Director of end user computing	Systems configuration
Disaster recovery	Technology rightsizing
End user support	Vendor partnerships

Keywords for manufacturing

Manufacturing is another industry with specific terminologies. Editing long-winded sentences and using key words makes your CV more powerful:

Asset management	Logistics manager
Assistant operations manager	Manufacturing engineer
Automated manufacturing	Materials co-ordinator
Capacity planning	On-time delivery
Cell manufacturing	Outsourcing
Cost reductions	Shipping and receiving operation
Distribution management	Spares and repairs management
Environmental health and safety	Union negotiations
Inventory control	Warehousing operations

Keywords for human resources

The Human Resources industry is all-embracing, from recruitment and selection through to payroll, performance management and redundancies. Using keywords to accurately describe your role is crucial:

Compensation surveys	Regulatory affairs
Diversity training	Sourcing
Grievance proceedings	Staffing
Job task analysis	Succession planning
Labour contract negotiations	Team leadership
Leadership development	Training specialist
Recruiter	Wage and salary administration

Knowing Where to Find Keywords

How can you find keywords for your occupation or career field? Use a highlighter to pluck keywords from these resources:

- ✔ **Online and printed help-wanted ads:** Highlight the job skills, competencies, experience, education and other nouns that employers ask for.

- ✔ **Job descriptions:** Ask employers for them, check at libraries for books or software with job descriptions, or search online. To find them online, just enter such terms as 'job descriptions' or 'job descriptions trainer' or 'job descriptions electrical engineer' on a search engine, such as Google (www.google.com).

- ✔ **Trade magazine news stories:** Text about your career field or occupation should be ripe with keywords.

- ✔ **Online or printed annual reports of companies in your field:** The company descriptions of key personnel and departmental achievements should offer strong keyword clues.

- ✔ **Programmes for industry conferences and events:** Speaker topics address current industry issues, a rich source of keywords.

- ✔ **Internet search engine:** Key in a targeted company's name and search the site that comes up. Look closely at the careers portal and read current press releases.

    You can also use Internet search engines to scout out industry-specific directories, glossaries and dictionaries.

Mining for keywords in job descriptions

The excerpts below of two job descriptions illustrate how you can find keywords almost everywhere. In these examples, the keywords are italicised.

Car Dismantler:

✔ Knowledge of proper operation of *lifts, forklifts, torches, power wrenches,* and so on.

✔ Knowledge of *warehouse, core* and *stack locations.*

✔ Skill to move *vehicles* without damaging vehicle, other vehicles or personnel.

✔ Skill to remove *body* and *mechanical parts* without damage to part, self or others.

✔ Ability to read a *Dismantler report* and assess *stock levels.*

✔ Ability to accurately assess condition of *parts* to be recorded.

Budget Assistant:

✔ Reviews *monthly expense statements,* monitors *monthly expenditures* and gathers supporting *documentation* for supervisor review and approval.

✔ Performs basic *arithmetic operations* to calculate and/or verify *expense totals* and *account balances.*

✔ Operates *computer* to enter data into *spreadsheet* and/or *database.* Types routine *correspondence* and *reports.*

✔ Operates office equipment such as *photocopier, fax machine* and *calculator.*

Getting a Grip on Grammar

CV language differs from normal speech in several ways. In general, keep the language tight and the tone professional.

Here are a few do's and don'ts of grammar:

✔ **Always use your own voice:** Don't say 'expeditious' when you want to say 'swift'.

✔ **Do not use first-person pronouns (I, we):** Your name is at the top of each CV page, so the recruiter knows it's about *you.* Eliminate first-person pronouns. Also, don't use third-person pronouns (he, she) when referring to yourself – the narrative technique makes you seem pompous. Simply start with a verb.

✔ **Avoid using articles (the, a, an):** Articles crowd sentences and don't clarify meaning. Substitute *retrained staff* for *retrained the staff.*

✔ **Substitute helping verbs (have, had, may, might):** Helping verbs weaken claims and credibility, implying that your time has passed and portraying you as a job-hunting weakling. Say *managed* instead of *have managed.*

✔ **Don't use passive 'being' verbs (am, is, are, was, were):** Being verbs suggest a state of existence rather than a state of motion. Try *monitored requisitions* instead of *requisitions were monitored.* The active voice gives a stronger, more confident delivery.

✔ **Don't shift tenses:** Use the present tense for a job you're still in and the past tense for jobs you've left. But, among the jobs you've left, don't switch back and forth between tenses. Another big mistake: dating a job as though you're still employed (2008–Present) and then describing it in the past tense.

✔ **Don't be long-winded:** Unless you keep your sentences lean and clean, readers won't take time to decipher them. Try processing this:

Reduced hospital costs by 67 per cent by creating a patient independence programme, where they make their own beds, and as noted by hospital finance department, costs of nails and wood totalled £300 less patient than work hours of maintenance staff.

Eliminate complex sentences by dividing ideas into sentences of their own and getting rid of extraneous details:

Reduced hospital costs by 67 per cent. Originated patient independence programme that decreased per-patient expense by £300 each.

✔ **Avoid abbreviations:** Abbreviations are informal and not universal – even when they're career-specific. Use *Internet* instead of *Net.*

The exception is industry jargon – use it, especially in digital CVs. Knowledge and use of industry jargon adds to your credibility to be able to correctly and casually use terms common to the industry in which you're seeking employment.

Spelling Like a Pro

What is the name of a CV self-defence manual for jobseekers? The dictionary!

Of all the reasons causing recruiters and hiring managers to shoot down CVs, carelessness with spelling, grammar and choice of words ranks close to the top. Even when the real reason for rejection is bias or something else entirely, as in 'I just don't like that bloke', the use of misspelled words is a convenient justification. Make sure you spell-check your CV before you print or upload it. And even if you use the computer's spell-check, read it again in case the automated system changes the words into something entirely different to what you want to put in your CV. Also, no matter how many skills you have to offer, sending a CV riddled with spelling mistakes may eliminate you straightaway from short-listing. Employers especially recoil from impaired spelling when the jobseeker botches the interviewer's or the organisation's name. (You can Google your way to the company's website to spell the organisation's name; you can call to confirm the spelling of the interviewer's name.) Here's the takeaway message:

Know the computer spell-checker. Know the dictionary, in print or online at dictionary.com. And know a human being who can carefully proofread your CV to pick up grammar mistakes or misused words.

Chapter 8

Catching the Eye in Three Seconds Flat

In This Chapter

▶ When three's not a crowd

▶ Open spaces to bounce your words

▶ Choosing design to impress

*O*ne of the most important marketing tools for your CV is the way you lay the document out. Imagine one person sitting at a desk with 400 CVs to read. They all look alike, words blurring into words, then Ahh! Your CV pops up, the paper feels good, your layout is attractive and this person opens two drooping eyes to rapt attention.

There are no hard and fast rules about the way you lay out your CV, but the first thing about design is to avoid clutter. The same rule that applies when someone is selling a house. This is not what you like personally, it's what works for the prospective employer or whoever chooses the CV from that huge pile. So the 'three-second' glance has to absorb a lot of information in a very short time: presentation, key words and the typeface you use.

Fortunately, you don't have to be techno savvy to pass the three-second glance. All you need is a basic knowledge of word processing and the guidelines we cover in this chapter.

Word Processing in a Nutshell

Hand-written CVs are as extinct as dinosaurs, but you don't have to own a computer or word-processing program to create your CV. You can access many public areas to produce your CV. That's good news because *all* CVs must be produced electronically. For example, you can go to thousands of Internet cafés for minimal amounts, your local library offers this free of charge, and some employment resources centres provide advice, typing and printing facilities.

The only instance in which you may be asked to hand-write a document is if the employer requests a covering letter in this format. Otherwise, everything is done via word-processing systems.

Make sure you write the CV by hand before you book space at these public areas so you that you can begin typing as soon as you get there and so save time.

The most commonly used word-processing package is Microsoft Word for Windows because it is compatible for most online and computer systems.

Three's a crowd – or not: CVs can be over a page

A common belief is that a CV has to be presented on only one or two pages, otherwise it is eliminated straight-away. Not so! For persons who have more than 10 years' experience in one profession, it is difficult to ditch the third or even fourth page because substantial detail may be lost.

Okay, you do have to edit copy and retain two pages if you find that just two lines of a paragraph are being printed on the third page. If, on the other hand, your relevant experience for the job you're applying for is demonstrated on Pages 2–3, never delete data to the detriment of your career history; just continue onto a third page and make sure the copy extends to at least halfway down.

You don't have to use Word, but if you opt for another program, don't use software that is obsolete, such as WordStar. Also avoid Microsoft Works; it is almost impossible for you to open the document later on if you use other computers that do not have the software. And avoid earlier versions of Mac computers unless they've been made compatible to Microsoft Office.

Never write all the contents of your CV in BLOCK LETTERS. It never works well for visual impressions. Use block letters to separate out your name, then use again when you write the sections, such as EMPLOYMENT or EDUCATION.

Printing Your CV

Before you print, make sure that your printer has ink or toner. You don't want to submit a CV that has dots or streaks across the page. When the employer skims the CV, she wants to see all the words in the places they should be, not pick up on strange dots scattered across the page or streaks of ink in slightly different shades.

The worst thing you want to do is present a CV that looks as if you're experimenting on canvas.

A potential employer also doesn't want to start reading a sentence, turn the page, and see that some contents have dropped off the page because the CV margins were set outside the printing parameters. This problem sometimes happens when people are rushing to get their applications into that post box before the last collection. You look at the computer, all seems fine with your hard-hitting CV, so you print with a flourish, staple the pages in sequence and congratulate yourself that you'll meet the deadline.

Speaking of margins, make sure all four margins of the page look even, even if you tweak the top and bottom ones for more space. This gives the impression that you've made an effort to present your CV in a professional manner. Try to use no lower than 1.5 cm from the edge of the margin.

Selecting Paper

As long as your CV is laid out properly, you're free to select any neutral colour paper – such as white, ivory or cream – to print your CV on.

Of course, some people go the extra step and use thick, water-marked paper. This extra touch is fine if you're sending your CV through the post directly to the Human Resources Department or Head of Personnel. However, using such expensive paper isn't practical when you're sending CVs to more than one person or as speculative documents. Not only is the practice expensive, but it doesn't have much effect. Sometimes, the CV is short-listed from an agency even before it reaches the employer's hands.

And never, never, no matter how inspired you feel as a designer, use those fancy and sometimes hideous page borders. The practice is so-not modern, and having thick, multi-layered borders around the page will just make the employer snort in annoyance.

Colour your CV neutral

Never get a stroke of genius and start printing your CV on pink, orange, baby-blue or any other 'my style' paper. One young extroverted graduate chose patterned paper with sunshine reminiscent of romantic nights under the Caribbean sun. He sent out at least 100 CVs for about two months and wondered why he did not get a response. Then he ran out of the exotic paper and disgruntled about his nostalgia for Montego Bay not being noticed, he used white paper for the CV. He landed a job after that.

Moral of the story: The employer does not want to find out about your favourite colour or mood. Emphasising your skills using neutral paper is quite adequate.

Being Consistent

A CV will always be effective if it remains consistent throughout the document. This means there are no shocks awaiting the reader such as finding a completely different format when she turns the page. In other words, if the potential employer loses the second page of your CV, she needs to be able to tell by the look and feel which page goes – or doesn't go – with the first page of your CV.

The following basic guidelines help ensure consistency:

- ✔ Use the same font for the entire document. You can use different sizes but remember to use them systematically. For instance, if you write your heading in 12 point, use that style throughout. If you write your job titles in bold lettering, do the same on all pages.

- ✔ Never mix the tabulation settings across the page. The most annoying thing for a prospective employer is to see copy across the page with too much tabulation at different sections. At a glance, this presentation looks haphazard – the employer may put the CV aside for further consideration and never come back to it. If you decide to write in a format left to right, with regular tabs, be consistent throughout the document. If you place a heading in the middle of the page, make sure to do this with all headings to the end of the CV because the employer, by the end of the first page, will have become used to this format and the eye bounces quickly.

- ✔ One crucial aspect to making your CV pass the three-second glance is to make sure the language you use is consistent. CVs are written in the formal first person without the prefixes. For example, instead of 'I was responsible for. . .' you write 'Responsible for. . .'. Maintain this style of language at all times, never lapse into 'My duties were. . .' or 'I did this or that. . .' It is imperative that you make sure your CV remains consistent when you revise it at different stages.

Excessive use of bullet points puts your CV into the high-risk category, that is, the risk of not being short-listed because the document is too cluttered. This is especially so if you use a bold format bullet style which simply makes the reader's eye become tired and perhaps triggers off some groan of annoyance. Use bullet points when you're giving your job summaries on one line. For example: 'Implemented two major projects with LUKOIL in Russia.' If you're writing a paragraph, forget it. The bullets will not have much effect as the whole purpose of using them is for easy and quick absorption of words.

Breaking It Up

Writing a CV also means that you lay out the information so as to grab attention straightaway. It does not make sense to edit your CV and have perfect copy and then place the contents in a manner that makes the document look dense. Break up the copy throughout the CV, and have enough white space for the reader to grab details as she scans the page.

White space is a term used to describe the volume of breaks you format your CV with. Two important tools help you create effective white space: the Return key and Tabulations. The Return key makes white space between the sections of the CV, the tabulation key creates space across the page.

At the top of the CV, you can use the Return key to make your name stand out by creating space between that line and your personal details. You do not have to write your middle name.

The most important section of the CV is the description you give for each job. This is where your 'transferable skills' are demonstrated, especially when you're shaping the CV for a position you do not necessarily have the experience for. The prospective employer who has vast experience of short-listing candidates automatically seeks information on your job titles and the duties you have/had. Make this copy flow by putting white space around it; do not strangle copy in blocks of details; do not be afraid to use the Return key. If you're running into more than two or three pages because you're making too many returns throughout the CV, first of all you revise the contents. When editing copy, avoid using superlative language like 'particularly' or 'simultaneously'. (For more on wording, see Chapter 7.)

Use concise, shorter sentences in a crisp manner. For instance, instead or writing 'I participated in team meetings, taking minutes and sending them to people', you could simply write 'Facilitated meetings'.

Choosing Typefaces and Font Size

Choosing the correct typeface is an important element to break up an otherwise dense CV. People who use word-processing packages usually gravitate towards certain typefaces because they get used to them. Similarly, the prospective employer becomes accustomed to reading certain typefaces on a CV and expects you to produce the document using one of them. Popular typefaces include Arial, Helvetica, Georgia, Times New Roman and Verdana.

Once you decide on the typeface you want to use, keep it throughout the CV. Never mix and merge type faces; this creates a chaotic visual impression.

Try to avoid typefaces which look as if you were writing with a quill in the Victorian age, such as Brush Script MT. These typefaces are difficult to read in large volumes; they'll slow down the reader from the offset and the CV may be eliminated even before she notices your name. Also, avoid using very bold, thick typefaces such as Arial Black or Britannia Bold. Imagine reading two to three pages of such copy. Headaches galore!

Use a font size that doesn't force the prospective employer to use a magnifying glass to read the contents. Never reduce the font size to less than 11 point on your CV, no matter which typeface you're using. Resist the temptation to reduce fonts if you realise you're exceeding two or three pages. Lazy, lazy, lazy. Go back over your contents and edit, edit, edit. (Besides, it's a myth that your CV must be only one page; see the sidebar earlier in this chapter.)

You do not have to write every single task you performed in a job. And you don't have to waffle on about your rugby success in secondary school if you're running out of space. It is better to sacrifice additional information and retain the font size than pad out your CV with irrelevant information. If you find that you're reducing the font because you have a page three that contains your interests and the fact that you've managed to keep a clean UK driving licence for the last four years, delete that information.

In some professions, a well-presented formal CV with lots of measured white space isn't so crucial. If you're applying for positions in advertising, the media, graphic design or the performing arts, the design can be more creative with more adventurous typefaces. However, even though your CV may pass the 'three second glance', it must sustain interest with clear, edited contents.

Chapter 9

CVs for Your Life's Changing Phases

In This Chapter

▶ Looking for a job in your golden years

▶ Returning to civilian life for service personnel

▶ Returning to work after having children

▶ Engineering a move into a prestige or higher civil service job

*A*t several points in the flow of your life, you're likely to find yourself in a 'just passing through' stage where you're temporarily required to come up with new solutions to employment roadblocks. At such stages, you're required to think differently about how to put your best foot forward.

In changing from one phase to another, whether in lifestyle or the working environment, revitalise your CV with strategies and techniques that will ease the transition. When faced with a new situation, remind yourself to sell solutions, not histories.

This chapter shows you how to adapt to changing trends in recruitment.

Grabbing Good Jobs When You're Older

If you're beyond 50 (maybe even 40 in today's world), it's pointless to debate whether or not age discrimination exists. It does. Society continues to wink at age bias even though the UK has anti-ageism legislation.

Of course, being a more mature jobseeker has its pluses along with its minuses.

The strengths of maturity

If you're an older jobseeker, you have at least five main selling points and a slew of minor ones:

- ✔ **You have more knowledge and greater wisdom than you did when you were half your age.** Your judgement is a valuable commodity. You may easily save an employer substantial 'mistake money' because you've seen most situations play out in some form over the course of your learning lifetime. You have the common sense that comes with experiencing life. You won't rush into hasty or rash decisions.

- ✔ **You're dependable.** You won't leave for frivolous reasons. Employers can rely on you showing up and doing the job as expected. You're more grateful for a good job than younger workers. You show your appreciation with a strong work ethic. Your work history shows that your word is your bond.

- ✔ **You're motivated to be flexible and adaptable.** You may value working less than a full-time schedule. You can adapt to the changing needs of a business.

- ✔ **You may be able to work for less money than your competition.** Your children are grown and your expenses are down.

- ✔ **You see the big picture in dealing with people.** You've had years to discover what makes them tick. You know from first-hand experience the quality that customer service consumers expect and appreciate.

Other positive characteristics you've acquired over time include the following: You've developed a taste for team playing because you've seen how all hands can work collectively for the good of a business. Unlike mountain-climbing younger employees, you won't skip out for a flashy opportunity when you've got a bird in hand – you're happy to be working and you've seen enough of the dot-com bubbles to last a lifetime.

The mature person's soft spots

The notion that older people have had their day and should make room for the next generation is deeply ingrained, say researchers. The stereotype is that you can't teach an old dog new tricks and that all mature workers are alike in their inability to learn, perform, energise, remember and deal with change in a new kind of world.

Here is a selection of prevalent myths about workers of a certain age, followed by the realities you need to try to reflect in your CV:

- ✔ **'Older workers can't or won't learn new skills.'** A smart, well-executed CV proves this bit of conventional wisdom wrong, as it certainly is: The over-50s crowd is the fastest growing group of Internet users. Use technical terms on your CV if appropriate. Mention new skills recently acquired. Studies show only negligible loss of cognitive function in people between 50 and 70.

- ✔ **'Training older workers is a lost investment because they won't be around for long.'** The life of a new technology for which workers are trained often won't last as long as the work life of an employee over 50. Find ways to tell employers that you

  - Are committed to doing quality work.

  - Can get along with co-workers and younger bosses.

  - Have strong skills in reading, writing and arithmetic.

  - Are someone who can be counted on in a crisis.

  - Are willing to be flexible about doing different tasks.

- ✔ **'Benefit and accident costs are higher for older workers.'** According to a recent study, older workers take fewer sick days per year than do other age groups because they have fewer acute illness and sporadic sick days. Although it's true that individual older workers' health, disability and life insurance costs do rise slowly with age, they are offset by lower costs because of fewer dependents.

Overall, fringe benefit costs stay the same as a percentage of salary for all age groups. Older workers take fewer risks in accident-prone situations and statistically have lower accident rates than other age groups. Handling this on a CV is tricky but you can say, if true: 'Robust health; no dependents other than spouse.'

To forestall age discrimination, tailor your CV to make yourself look like a well-qualified candidate, not a well-preserved one, by using the following tips:

- ✔ **Match your target job description.** Find or write job descriptions of your target occupations. If you like your current field and are leaving involuntarily because it's disappearing from under your feet, start with job descriptions in closely related jobs. Compare requirements of related jobs with your transferable skills profile. If you don't like your current field, forget we mentioned it.

  Knowing what you have to offer gets you up off your knees, out of the past, and into the future; it enables you to write a CV that readers will respect, by saying, 'This is what I can do for you that will add to your productivity, efficiency or effectiveness.'

- ✔ **Shorten your CV.** The general guideline is, 'Go back no more than 10 years.' But if that doesn't work for the job you seek, one answer is to create a functional CV in which you emphasise your relevant skills in detail towards the top of the CV and downplay overly impressive titles that may intimidate younger employers. For example, *Senior Vice President, Sales* becomes *Sales Executive.*

- ✔ **Focus your CV.** Concentrate on highlighting your two most recent or most relevant jobs. Don't attempt to give equal attention to each of your past jobs. If your job experience has been diverse, your CV may look like a job-hopping tale of unrelated job after unrelated job.

- ✔ **Show that you're a tower of strength.** Give examples of how you solved problems, recovered expenses and learned to compensate for weaknesses in your working environment. Emphasise how quickly such adjustments occurred. More mature people who've survived a few fallen skies are valuable assets in difficult times.

✔ **Demonstrate political correctness.** This is especially important for positions that have contact with the public. Show that you're familiar with contemporary values by using politically correct terms wherever appropriate. Examples include *diversity, cross-cultural, mainstream, multi-ethnic, people with disabilities* (never *handicapped*), and *women* (not *girls*).

✔ **Distribute your CV online.** Doing so helps dispel any ideas that you're over the hill. See Part I for more on digital CVs.

✔ **Omit ancient education dates.** Of course, the absence of dates sends a signal: This is a geezer who read a CV book. But at least it shows that you have sufficient faculties left to read the book and play the game.

✔ **Trim your CV.** For very experienced professionals, sorting out the most powerful CV points can be difficult. It's like being a gifted child – so many choices and you're good at all of them! You know what they say, though: 'The longer the cruise, the older the passengers'.

✔ **Use appropriate headings.** If you're using freelance, hobby or volunteer experience, use the heading *Work Experience* and list it first, unless you have changed your focus through education. If so, begin with the heading *Education.* To refine this heading, substitute your target-job-related education, such as *Accounting Education* or *Healthcare Education.* Your employment history follows.

What do you do with all the experience that was great in your old job but means nothing where you want to go? Lump it together at the end of your CV under *Other Experience* or *Earlier Experience.* Limit it to positions, titles, employers and/or degrees and educational institutions. If extraneous experience is older than five years, squash it entirely.

A lower-level job beckons

At some point in your life, you may take a deep breath, stare out of the office window and decide that you need to change your career. Whatever the reason, the most important thing is to identify the possibilities for smooth transition into another field. Sometimes you have to compromise on salary because you may be starting from scratch in that industry.

Show skills as they apply to a new position

Making a career change? As you list your skills, competencies, education and experience, lead with the information relevant to the new position and then list the other data. You have to quickly convince the employer that you have the ability to handle the position.

Assume an engineer wants to move into sales. The CV needs to mention things like 'client liaison', 'preparing presentations for meetings', and 'strong communications skills'.

You may begin by writing: 'Used a strong technical background and excellent communications skills in a sales role.' Then continue to speak of your ability to provide good technical advice in a business relationship.

Writing that you 'enjoy learning' is a coin with two sides; the employer may see you as flexible in your desire to further your education or, conversely, make a negative judgement that you don't have the skills right now to hit the ground running.

When you're willing to step down from your previous level of work, don't try to do it with a CV. Do it by a personal first contact so that you get a chance to colour your positioning in the best hue, and to defuse intuitive rejection. Tell your story before recruiters and employers can say they don't want to hear it.

Positioning your status counts. You aren't a manager lowering yourself by looking for a much less responsible job. You're a career changer exploring new fields.

Go directly to the recruitment manager and explain your reasoned willingness to accept lower remuneration:

> *I have a great work attitude and excellent judgement. Show me a new task, and I get it right away. I understand, of course, that the trade-off in moving into your industry is less pay and responsibility.*

When you've opened the door, hand over your CV. You need breathing room to shape your CV in a way that spotlights your transferable skills as they pertain to the job you seek –

such as a talent for working with numbers, reliability, and a good attendance record, as well as fast-learning ability.

Employment in the autumn years

When you have a long job history, you're more likely to need updates on the following issues.

- **Choosing the wrong focus.** Choosing the wrong focus is a problem shared with new graduates (see Chapter 10) who fail to identify those jobs that are the best path to the hoped-for next job. Like the estate agent's adage that the operating principle is 'location, location, location', the operating principle for the better jobs is 'target, target, target'. Present your CV in a manner that makes the employer quickly see your skills relevant to the position you're applying for, instead of having to wade through reverse chronological data and not find important details on the first page.

- **Revealing age negatively.** Don't blurt out your age. Don't put old education first on your CV (unless you're a professional educator). Avoid listing jobs with dates older than 10 or 15 years. If you must include dusty jobs, de-emphasise the dates or omit them. You can summarise old jobs under a heading of 'Prior to 20XX' and avoid being too specific. Alternatively, you can include all jobs under functional headings. Try not to describe older jobs in detail.

- **Appearing low-tech.** Some seasoned professionals who do not have computers still type CVs; others with computers have old-fashioned dot matrix printers. Their CVs are often stopped at the door. Today's readers like crisp, attractive layouts that only a computer and laser printer can create. (For more on creating a sharp layout, see Chapter 8.)

- **Not supplementing secondary school education.** If your highest education attainment is secondary school, don't forget to mention any continuing education, including seminars and workshops related to your work, if it applies to what you want to do next.

Working after nurturing

If you gave up full-time employment to take care of children, returning to the workplace can be daunting, especially if you took a career break for more than five years. Your heart starts beating faster at the mention of video conferencing or when someone talks about Microsoft Outlook.

First consider what kind of job you want. What skills do you have after so many years away from the buzz of the workplace? You may want to start off gently with some voluntary work in an office or with a company relevant to the career you want to resume.

On your CV, make sure to put information about activities you've fulfilled during those years you went to the Toddlers Group. Did you volunteer in your children's school, for example, being on the Board of Governors, or organising fund-raising stints? Did you complete any form of part-time work, say administration for the family business or writing for a local publication?

If you've not taken part in any outside activities, remember that keeping a household budget is a transferable skill. On your CV, you may want to put a sentence: High level of numeracy with ability to control stringent budgets.

Winning Interviews as a New Civilian

If you're leaving the military and looking for a civilian job, pay attention to this section. It shows you how best to present your military experience as you look for a civilian job.

Making military strengths count

You have a chest full of selling points. Here are six super marks of merit:

- ✔ You have exceptionally good training. Military training at any level is recognised as being superior for mental and physical discipline, and you've shown that you're trainable.

✔ You have substantial real-life experience. You may have things like high-tech and leadership skills that you acquired at an early age and that are not typically available to the civilian workforce. Maybe you were in charge of a troop and even advanced to a position responsible for policymaking and strategic planning.

✔ You know how to be a team player and show up on time. You perform well under pressure. You know how to accomplish assignments in a structured organisation.

✔ You may have experience with something directly relevant to the civilian job market: operations management, supply chain procurement, human resource management, systems administration or financial planning.

✔ You have a strong work ethic to get it right the first time.

✔ You're flexible and able to quickly adapt to changing situations.

Dealing with military soft spots

Poor communication is the biggest reason recruiters or hiring managers overlook well-qualified military candidates. They just don't get what your CV says when you speak military-ese, not civilian-ese.

When you've finished writing your CV, put it through the civilian translation wringer by asking friends and neighbours who know nothing about things military to read it and see whether they understand what you're talking about.

Admittedly, some employers do believe in a stigmatised stereotype of military service members as being rough, tough, rigid and hard-headed types whose idea of leadership is command and control. A CV won't do much to alter that perception but if it's well done, it will help get you inside an interview room where your pleasing personality may be able to reverse false, preconceived notions.

Here are other CV pointers to boost your cause.

✔ **Advertise what you're selling.** Avoid building your CV around your military rank or title. Instead, emphasise the qualifications you bring to the employer.

✔ **Consider your best format.** A targeted CV (Chapter 5) is a good choice, say many career coaches who work with ex-military personnel, because it features competencies and skills in professional categories, rather than a chronological history by rank or job title. But this doesn't mean a reverse chronological CV format can't be used to your advantage.

If you're working with a third-party recruiter, do as the recruiter – who is carrying your immediate future in his hands – advises.

✔ **Hone in on job fairs.** Job fairs are among the most potent employment avenues by which service members and veterans can meet employers, network, and even be interviewed on the spot.

Don't insert your National Insurance number, keep it off your CV, cover letter, or application form. If you suspect that your data has been compromised, ward off identity theft by monitoring your credit reports and putting a fraud alert or a freeze on your credit accounts.

✔ **Search through Google, making sure you ask to find the UK pages.** Look for 'vacancies for military personnel' or 'close protection vacancies in the UK'. Many military officers transfer their skills for civilian life into close protection of politicians and others.

Government Hopefuls: From Private to Public

Switching from the corporate world into a civil service position is sometimes difficult because of the different recruitment practices. Imagine producing a highly competitive CV and getting ready to search for a civil service job. You access the public and not-for-profit sector job website at www.jobsgopublic.com and then realise you have to fill in an application form instead!

Most central and local government departments recruit by application forms and won't accept a CV, no matter how well written and how much it reflects your transferable skills into the sector. The same applies to community sector organisations and charities.

Presenting short-term work on your CV

Mature people may be doing work for a specific company but being paid through a temp agency or other intermediary and so are unsure about how to report the information on their CVs. You don't have to list the middleman firm. Note only the companies for which the work was performed. Here's a brief template:

Company A, Company B, Company C
[date] to present

For **Company A,** Name of Department/ Division

As **job title,** performed:

✔ achievement

✔ achievement

✔ achievement

For **Company B,** Name of Department/ Division

As **job title,** implemented:

✔ achievement

✔ achievement

✔ achievement

For **Company C,** Name of Department/ Division

As **job title,** credited with:

✔ achievement

✔ achievement

✔ achievement

P.S. If your job titles are extreme and insignificant or overly exalted, don't bold them.

However, some senior positions require CVs, such as Business Development directors or heads of IT and Business Analyses. On the whole though, be prepared to fill in application forms (see Chapter 10 on Application Forms processes).

When applying for civil service jobs, avoid using industry jargon such as 'executive coaching' or 'team player'. Replace with 'devised training programmes' or 'worked within cross-functional teams'. Remember that the public and community sectors use less hard-hitting terminology than the private sector, which is based on profitability and competitiveness. Recruiters are more interested in whether you have the skills to deliver presentations to 'partner organisations' rather than to 'stakeholders'. They're more interested in whether you communicate with 'people from diverse communities' rather than an 'international clientele'.

When targeting the public sector, replace the words that seem too bombastic: 'executed projects' (delivered projects); 'spearheaded' (oversaw); 'orchestrated' (managed). It may be useful to subscribe to a specialist agency that recruits for civil service positions and ask consultants to appraise the CV so that the tone is correct for the public sector.

Chapter 10

Nabbing a Job as a New Graduate

In This Chapter

▶ Using your experience (or lack of it!) to grab that graduate programme

▶ Landing the job with or without experience

▶ Wading through competency-based application forms

*O*kay, so you're feeling on top of the world. You just graduated, flashed back to three years of late night swotting and drinking budget coffee to stay awake, and printed out the CV from the Careers' Office at uni. Where do you go from here?

If you're like many students, you've worked in *stop-gap* positions, typically ad hoc duties within hospitality, administration or customer relations, or held summer work placements or work experience in your vocation while you studied. In this chapter, we explore how you can use these opportunities to enhance your chances of employment. We also give you tips in case you have no experience at all, never worked in a commercial setting and never had a 'stop-gap' job.

Getting Your Foot in the Door

You're in demand, you're a graduate and hundreds of international and specialist corporations are waiting to snap you up. They are everywhere, on billboards, in glossy magazines you read, in the newspapers, online and on the television.

You sigh to yourself and wish you could get a foot in the door of one of these corporations; after all, this is the reason you chose the degree course.

The good news is that thousands of international corporations use online methods to run graduate recruitment programmes. You're required to submit your CV/covering letter, or fill in application forms with specific questions and mini-psychometric tests. (For more on completing application forms, see the section 'Wading through the Maze of Graduate Application Forms' later in this chapter.)

You can use the Internet to discover which corporations are recruiting at this time, the criteria they are using to short-list and the offers they have to attract graduates. Use a search phrase through Google such as: 'companies offering graduate programmes' or 'companies offering training programmes'. Both types of programmes are similar in nature: you get your foot in the door, you rub shoulders with very experienced teams, gain insight into the profession and, depending on performance, after six months to a year you may be whisked off to the USA or Singapore to start charting that career you so wanted during your coffee-filled vigils.

Apply to companies that offer graduate positions most suited to your degree. In the event you wish to take a break from hearing all that jargon for awhile, you can apply to companies which offer appointments as a management consultant or customer relations executive, or a host of other titles. In this way you establish contact with and build up a portfolio with all sorts of customers – and it's not as involved as being a business analyst or a taxation officer!

Revising and Drafting Your CV

With your hit list of corporations, examine your own CV to see whether it stands out. One way of making your CV stand out is to insert a 'Key Skills' category right below your personal details. Write this category with great care, making sure that you list the skills required for the Graduate Programme. For instance, if the criteria require an honours degree graduate, start your Key Skills category with: 'Honours graduate in Bio-medicine' or 'Honours degree in Marketing and Sales'.

No work experience, no voluntary work?

For you graduates who chose to relax during the summer holiday, your CV will comprise mainly academic data. After writing your personal details and Key Skills, you place your qualifications first. You can also list the key modules you completed in the last two years at uni to make the CV longer. You have no experience of paid work – but did you assist in the family business? Put it in! You do not even have to let the employer know that it was the family business until you go to the interview. If your family does not have a business, what about voluntary work or self-development projects? Some graduates have travelled abroad during their studies and may have become involved in charity work. Put it in.

Right, your family does not have a business and you did not bother with charity work or self-development. However, you may have participated in extracurricular activities at university, such as being the chair of the fund-raising society or the Students' Union representative. This kind of detail always looks good on the CV and shows you're a team player, you take initiative or you're just plain willing to exercise your natural leadership skills.

If you have no work experience at all, neither at uni nor in the commercial world, your CV then becomes a one-page document with only your Personal Details and Qualifications. You could insert the residual 'Additional Information' category where you mention awards, scholarships or languages.

Draft the list with about five crisp sentences across the page; for example, 'First-rate analytical skills with ability to assimilate data and create solutions'. That sentence will always impress a potential employer and it is generic for all graduates. Remember, you've completed detailed group and individual projects at university, and you've collated and interpreted complex details and designed presentations in order to get your marks. Remember also, the employer, no matter what profession you're aiming to climb the ladder in, expects some degree of analytical skills, whether innate or acquired.

In that list of Key Skills, include fluency or proficiency in any language. The world is evolving into one global market, especially with emerging economies such as Asia, the Middle East and Far East forcing attention outside of Europe and North America. If you have knowledge of some of the not-so-popular languages, such as Urdu, Arabic and Cantonese, emphasise this fact.

Next, begin enhancing your experience (or lack of it)! Graduate programmes are geared towards you acquiring commercial experience, so you're not expected to have much experience in the profession. However, think of the next person, who may have completed work experience during the previous summer holidays while you were basking in the South of France. (If that's your situation, make sure that you check out the sidebar 'No work experience, no voluntary work?') How do I compete against this person? Well, the next category on your CV is 'Professional/Qualifications'. Here, you insert details of your degree course and the university you attended. You must also include the key modules relevant to the position and sometimes the topic of your dissertation.

Don't elaborate too much on the project you received top marks for. Stating the title of the project and perhaps two sentences on what it entailed is fine. Don't make the mistake of informing the employer what technologies you used, the different stages and how many team members were involved in the project. This type of detail is sometimes highly technical and slows down the momentum of the CV. By the time the employer trawls through what you did, how you did it and the outcome, the CV is moving towards the middle of the page and she's yawning.

The next category must help to 'sell your skills'. Were you one of the steadfast students who secured work experience last summer, meaning you can now write about having some insight into the industry? Or did you prefer to take life easy in preparation for the gruelling final year?

Case Study: Landing the Job with Experience

In this section, you find out how to make the Graduate CV competitive by looking at how Lee Bramble, a freckle-faced graduate, hit the right chords two weeks after he left university. We can also presume that Mr Bramble has progressed up the corporate ladder and now has a silver name plate on his oak door, thanks to his remarkable CV, shown in Figure 10-1!

LEE BAMBLE

66 Queen Anne Road
Charles Dickens House
Woodside, London 23T
Contact No: 00000 000000
E-mail: leebamble@netmail.com

KEY SKILLS

Honours graduate in Computer Systems Engineering
Sound experience in project management in diverse industries
Ability to motivate colleagues and achieve significant results
Ability to work on own initiative under pressure and to set targets
Extensive knowledge of programming and associated systems
Excellent interpersonal and negotiating skills – at all levels
Adapt well to challenges; resilient and tenacious

PROFESSIONAL/QUALIFICATIONS

2001–2004	**Bolton University**	
		Bachelor of Engineering (Hons 2:2)
		- Computer Systems Engineering
		Core Modules:
		Programming & Software Design; Network Design & Advance Security; Internet Technology, OO Software Design; Computer Control & Interfacing; Data Network Services and Security
2000–2001	**Bristol University**	
		Foundation in Computing and Mathematics
		Computing (A); Electronics 1&2 (A, A); Mathematics 1 & 2 (A, C); Communication Systems (A); Introductory Science Technology (A); Physics (A)
Sept 1999–June 2000	**Green Park College**	
		Five GCSE subjects (A–C grades)

EMPLOYMENT SUMMARY

June 2003–Date   **Flatters Ltd**
Mortgage Broker
High volume of liaison with corporate and private clients, issuing information/advice as to diverse mortgage packages, recommending most appropriate services in

---

Figure 10-1: A CV for a graduate with experience.

accordance with clients' financial viability and relaying information on current market/economic trends affecting the market.

Undertook ad-hoc duties in designing/maintaining clients' HTML, JavaScript, XML, ASP and CSS based websites. Assisted in transition of manual records to computerised systems via SQL software. Devised/delivered training programmes to colleagues on proper use of the systems, and monitored efficiency to compile reports to senior management.

June 2001–Oct 2002   **Planet 19 Studio**
Receptionist
Coordinated daily administrative workload, implementing quality assurance policies and ensuring smooth operation at all times. Produced correspondence, disseminated information throughout the premises as well as externally and handled telephone queries. Carried out hospitality duties, greeting visitors and facilitating seminars/meetings. General administrative tasks.

PERSONAL INFORMATION

Date of Birth: January 14, 1982
Full, clean UK driver license
Interests include PC maintenance (enjoy building computers for friends/family members), snooker, table tennis and bowling.

REFERENCES AVAILABLE UPON REQUEST

Figure 10-1 *(continued)*

Why did Lee get the job and is now gazing through his glass window in Canary Wharf? He hit all the right points in each section of his CV:

- ✔ **Key skills:** Professional and academic skills are written first; general skills come at the end of the list. For instance, you may start the Key Skills box with 'Honours graduate in Business and Finance', and follow it with 'Some experience in initiating small strategic programmes in diverse fields'. Then you mention your analytical and communication skills and the fact that you work well on your own initiative or under pressure. You may put your languages at the end of the list so that they stand out, especially if you're applying for a position in the European regions or Asia and you have working knowledge of some languages in those countries.

✔ **Professional/qualifications:** This section includes full information about Lee's academic achievements. Elaborate on key modules and never put all modules from the First Year. Most graduates just allude to the final four modules and this is satisfactory.

✔ **Employment summary:** Many graduates have worked in different fields to supplement their studies. For instance, some work in bars, cafés, shops – especially if they made a mistake with their predicted budget and began feeling pangs of hunger after a few months. If you undertook some activities relating to your degree course, always remember to describe these. It makes a difference, as you see with Lee's CV. If your work was only remotely connected, and involved serving beverages and listening to people as they sought solace at the bottom of a wine glass, simply state the date, job title and place of employment.

✔ **Personal information:** Choose the information you want to provide. Examples of information: current UK driving licence; your hobbies; and if you wish, because you're deemed to be in the employable age group, you can state your date of birth. You may want to include your nationality, especially if the position will be located in the country you were born in. Otherwise, you choose what to say or you can omit the section completely.

✔ **References available:** Usually available upon request. If you don't have any work experience, use two academic references – tutors or course supervisors at your university. Make sure to ask permission before you start applying for jobs. Data Protection regulations advise you not to include full personal details of referees, especially if you're applying to online graduate recruitment programmes. Employers usually offer you the job, pending 'satisfactory references'. At this stage, you provide personal details of your referees.

Turning irrelevant employment into useful skills

For a graduate, all employment skills are useful, no matter how irrelevant you may believe they are. If for example, you worked as a sales consultant at a High Street shop and you're applying for a different kind of position, your interpersonal skills need to be emphasised. 'Liaised with various people, often minimising conflict'. This is relevant to the workplace. Or, if you worked as a waitress in a High Street wine bar, you may add that you cashed up at the end of business or implemented health and safety or security policies. Never assume that the employer does not want to know about the skills you acquired in these positions.

If you have no experience at all, you may consider, as said before, writing about your awards or positions of responsibility at uni.

Case Studying: Nabbing the Job When You Have No Experience

New graduate Becky Dolittle landed a job in the Finance sector, despite the fact that she has no experience in that sector, no experience in any working environment, no family business to run in the summer holidays and no voluntary work. How? She emphasised all the right elements in her CV, shown in Figure 10-2.

Becky emphasised her strong academic accolades from the offset, writing about the Honours degree and her general skills in the Key Skills box. And she mentioned her languages because she's applying for a position with an international investment corporation.

Note also that she listed all grades from secondary school to show consistency in academic excellence. In her Additional Information section, she cleverly wrote about her involvement with the Girl Guides and the awards she received.

BECKY DOLITTLE
Anytown, London
SE00 00
Tel: 000 00 000
Email: becky@hmail.com

KEY SKILLS
- Bachelor of Arts honours degree in Accountancy and Economics
- Ability to work on own initiative and to challenging deadlines
- Ability to motivate team members to achieve significant results
- Effective communication and interpersonal skills at all levels
- Practical knowledge of Microsoft Series and associated software
- Adapt well to challenges; resourceful and innovative
- Basic French, conversational German

PROFESSIONAL / QUALIFICATIONS

2004-2008	**The Financial Institute**
	Bachelor of Arts (Hons 2:1) –
	Accounting and Economics
	Key modules:
	Accounting Principles; Taxation;
	Human Resources in Finance;
	Management of Budgets
2003-2004	**Oaklands College**
	CACHE Diploma in Childcare and Education (Double A)
	AS English; German; Mathematics
2001-2003	**Oaklands College**
	NCFE Practical Craft Skills
	Key Skills (Communications) L3
	Early Years First Aid (St Johns Ambulance)
	Basic Counselling; Food Hygiene
1994-2001	**Bishop's Hatfield Girls' School**
	GCSE subjects: German (A); French (A);Mathematics (B); Resistant
Materials (B); English Literature/Language (Double Award C); Geography (C)

ADDITIONAL INFORMATION
I have been a Guide/Senior Section Guider and also have been Treasurer for both. I also work with the Brownies and volunteered with a Barnados befriending scheme for a year. Guiding Qualifications are:
Baden Powell Award (2/1999)
Duke of Edinburgh Award (Bronze/Gold)
Senior Section Camp Permit & Overnight Permit (7/2000)
Guide Leadership Qualification (Warrant)
Queens Guide Award (at a similar level to DoE Gold)

I enjoy reading non-fiction, biographies and magazines, especially those relating to history or geography.

REFERENCES AVAILABLE UPON REQUEST

Figure 10-2: A CV for a graduate with no experience.

Wading through the Maze of Graduate Application Forms

So you've done your CV, gone through the list of companies and you're ready to start hitting the Upload button – and then you realise you need to fill in an application form. Not only do you need to fill in a form but there may be some strange questions you need to answer too.

Is there a sinister twist to this graduate stuff? Why do you need my most significant achievement within the last three years? Hmm, is it that I have survived uni without starving to death and got top marks? Or, must I mention the fact that I swam in the English Channel and overcame my fear of a broad expanse of moving water?

Facing the harsh reality

Ninety-nine per cent of graduate application forms are designed to get vital personal information on you, particularly because employers want to see 'potential' for performing well in the job. Okay, you may believe baring your soul about having difficulties in completing your group project isn't nec-essary, but competency-based questions are based on mini-aptitude *tests*. This means that the employer does not only wish to know about your academic brilliance, but how you might cope in the workplace, whether you're a team player or if you can take a project and run with it without having to seek guidance all the time.

Employers designed these questions purposefully to glean the information they need as they have preconceived ideas about type of people they want to fill positions and their questions are designed to shortlist the right candidates.

Ninety per cent of graduates have no work experience in the vocations they pursued at university. Many of them have worked in 'stop-gap' positions, typically ad hoc duties within hospitality, administration or customer relations.

Getting your mind in gear

Although you don't need a CV to complete an application form, make a rough draft. Though the process differs, the application form has to be written in the same formal, crisp and concise language as the CV. Categories such as Personal Details, Education/Training and Employment Summary are straightforward. The difficulty comes when you begin filling in 'example questions' or 'scenario' illustrations.

It's obvious that answering application form questions cannot be done by just looking at your CV and repeating information presented there. You'll have to think about situations at work, during studies or in your personal life. Use examples drawn primarily from your work experience.

If, however, you've more substantial results as a voluntary worker or student, use these examples. For example, you worked in a newsroom every summer while pursuing a BA in Journalism. You carried out mundane tasks that had no relevance to writing news stories or interviewing the local mayor on environmental issues. At the same time, you also ended up in a local charity as a volunteer, writing press releases for social events, researching topics and liaising with external agencies. These voluntary duties are far more important than the work experience you undertook.

 Remember that employers seek practical, 'hands-on' skills even though you're accessing them through a graduate recruitment programme. While they are aware that academic pursuits may have taken up a significant portion of your time within the last three years, they'll be more impressed if you've undertaken some work experience and acquired a certain amount of working skills.

Moving into the maze of questions and answers

Ninety-nine per cent of competency-based questions have restrictions on the number of words you're allowed to respond with. The key to giving competitive answers is to deliberate on the response for a while and write the data down, concentrating on what you did, how you did it and the outcome. When you have these three important elements, you can edit the contents to the number of words required.

In this section, we look at how a graduate who has had some experience in paid and voluntary work responds to sample questions , compared to the answers of an inexperienced candidate. The answers were limited to a maximum of 200 words.

Describe a time when you worked well and achieved success with a group of others. What was the outcome? What was your contribution?

Experienced candidate's answer:

I was member of a voluntary team of undergraduates who organised and facilitated electronic workshops and seminars for new students having difficulties in using laboratory equipment such as oscilloscopes, spectrum analysers and simulators. We had planning meetings on how to develop the programme with tasks allocated to each member. I was responsible for booking the laboratory sessions, monitoring students' progress and devising individual programmes to raise levels of achievement. At the end of each programme, lecturers informed the group that the students were much more informed about equipment, and practical competency had significantly increased.

Inexperienced candidate's answer:

I am accustomed to being an integral team member. I am also aware that teamwork is vital for business objectives to be met at all times. On one occasion, whilst appointed Guide Leader, I co-ordinated a project on change implementation. This involved consulting with all persons on new procedures to be adopted within two months of notification from the Girl Guides' Association. The project was challenging because I had to include feedback from more than 36 girl guides who were located in different areas. Firstly, I held a meeting with my colleagues to accurately interpret the guidelines and delegated tasks to disseminate the information to all girl guides in different locations.

Secondly, I convened with all groups and again delegated tasks for us to successfully set a programme in accordance to the new rules. As a result of my personal innovation, the project was completed on time.

Most competency-based questions involve three elements: what the situation was, what you did and what the outcome was. In these examples, both candidates made sure to first of all, follow the three-step principle, then edit the answers afterwards.

Describe one of your biggest challenges where you had to persevere to succeed. What happened and what did you learn from this?

Experienced candidate's answer:

As a mortgage adviser, I was faced with the possibility of a sales agreement being abandoned because the vendor withdrew the advertised property at the last stages of the process, after the purchaser's offer had been accepted and during the period when a deposit was to be processed. The purchaser was frustrated by the action, having already prepared for relocation to the property and having made personal changes of lifestyle to accommodate this.

I liaised extensively with the vendors' representatives, including estate agents, in an attempt to rescind the decision. Unfortunately, negotiations were without avail. I then had to make an immediate decision to inform the purchaser of the stalemate. Before doing this, I researched similar properties in that location with similar specifications/budgets, as the purchaser had requested, and relayed these details to him. The situation was resolved because I had been successful in identifying alternative properties for the purchaser to make a choice.

Inexperienced candidate's answer:

I was appointed leader of the Planning Committee at my local Church to arrange a charity dinner and dance at an appropriate venue with accommodation for 80 persons. Firstly, I held a meeting with the four selected members to discuss how we will execute the project. I identified the different stages to be carried out, from securing the venue, costing the event, to disseminating information to all workers. Secondly, I delegated tasks to each member and set deadlines. I had to find a venue, negotiate the costs and appraise Health/Safety conditions. Colleagues arranged the programme, designed invitations and distributed them to Church members. The planning group drafted a list of all tasks and agreed amongst ourselves which team member would undertake specific tasks and deadlines of these.

One week before the event, we received unexpected notification that the venue would become unavailable on that day due to technical setbacks. I decided the dinner and dance should be held on the same day as specified, considering persons had already earmarked that date and re-arranged their schedules. I negotiated with six possible venues before delegating staff to inform customers. All was rectified and the event was very successful. I became more confident about my skills as result of this achievement.

What motivated you to apply to this company?

Experienced candidate's answer:

I became interested in applying for the Network Rail Graduate programme because of the company's recruitment policies, which seem to be flexible, accommodating candidates from diverse cultural and ethnic backgrounds. The company also offers a very wide range of graduate opportunities and there is no complexity in recruitment procedures, as against other corporations.

Also, the fact that the organisation is a private company limited by guarantee allows for confidence in its equal opportunities and quality assurance policies, compared to similar groups which may be structured on profitability, often at the expense of service delivery. Network Rail, on the other hand, has structured mechanisms with directors and there is safeguard for candidates who apply from diverse backgrounds.

Inexperienced candidate's answer:

Casa Lora is a highly reputed global institution with a solid track record. It has won many awards for excellence across different divisions, and has grown from a German commercial bank into a universal investment bank. I am particularly impressed that Casa Lora won the prestigious IFR's 2003 'Bank of the Year' award. I believe that the industry's finest people work at its Global Market Division, and the success in my application to Casa Lora would enhance my opportunities to pursue long-term aspirations in fixed income trading.

I have nurtured an avid interest in investment banking from an early age and wish to utilise transferable skills in other areas to secure placement at Casa Lora.

When you initially draft your answer, do not be concerned with the maximum number of words allowed. Write as many details as you wish before editing for word count. If you're allowed to answer in 200 words and have written only 120, do not attempt to 'pad' out the answers. It is better to have answered precisely rather than be perceived as waffling without meaning.

Wrapping up this competency-based question maze

Don't become confused by the questions. Read them through several times and you will then realise what the employer is asking you. So, in a nutshell:

> ✔ **You may be asked to answer three to six questions.** Think about your own background. Did you take up some work in the industry within the last two years? Or, did you have another job but you used your great personality and interpersonal skills to resolve issues with difficult people? Like someone screaming that the shoes she ordered online are much smaller than she wants and the colour is wrong. Or, did you get involved in a local charity and walk 20 miles to raise funds?

> ✔ **You'll definitely be asked to answer in a maximum number of words.** Usually, you're asked to answer in 200 to 500 words. Make sure you adhere to this rule – use your Word Count once you've edited the waffle and made it more concise and targeted.

Always, always, save your work every ten minutes while you complete online application forms! Some forms allow you to save some sections before you exit and start again after you've refreshed your brains. Others won't allow you to continue to the other section unless you've completed the one you're struggling with. Make sure no time limit exists before you log in and sit staring at the computer waiting for inspiration to set in. The best solution is to type and edit information in RTF and, once you are into the form online, cut and paste.

Chapter 11

The Bare Essentials of a Cover Letter

In This Chapter

▶ Knowing why you need a cover letter

▶ Exploring the different types of cover letters

▶ Writing a winning document

*M*ore and more employers are asking candidates to write cover letters with their applications. This practice has become increasingly popular over the last six years. The good news is that writing a letter is easy if you draft your CV first because you can use the contents of the CV in shorter form for the letter, maintaining the same style. (If you haven't created your CV yet, see Chapter 5.)

In this chapter, we tell you everything you need to know to write powerful, concise cover letters that will win you the interview.

Why Cover Letters Are Important

The cover letter is as important as the CV, and some employers even use this document to initially short-list candidates. Some employers just ask you to provide one because they assume this is the correct way to recruit candidates. Whatever their reasons for asking you to write one, make sure you do so and don't simply send the CV because you assume this is all that's necessary.

If you're asked to submit a cover letter with your CV, make sure to do so or you might be eliminated at the first stage of the envelope being opened.

If you submit applications in the more traditional manner involving stamps and post boxes, the cover letter is vital. This is usually the first document pulled from the envelope, and the recruiter forms a quick opinion on whether you're suitable for the job.

For tech-savvy people uploading CVs on numerous websites, the letter attachment must remain on one page. It is a cruel, cold world, this recruitment process, so at all times, make sure you're maximising your chances with a well-written cover letter and CV.

Never annoy the employer about how wonderful the company is or with details on your personal interests unless these are relevant. For instance, it is corny when you waffle on about having spent three months in the Himalayas on a sabbatical and how refreshed you are, ready to climb the corporate ladder with fresh air in your lungs. (However, if you're applying for a job with the Territorial Army, this detail might become relevant – well, without the bit about fresh air and climbing ladders.)

Getting Started with Definitions

There are generally two types of cover letters. If you're replying to an advertisement which says simply, 'Please submit a cover letter with your CV' or 'Send cover letter and CV', you will complete a *general cover letter*. If on the other hand, you're asked to provide details of your current salary, the reason you wish to have the position, or what skills you can bring to the company, you will write a *specific cover letter*.

> ✔ **General cover letter:** This is a standard one-page document that can be modified as you click and upload your CV or send out applications. With the generic letter, the body of the document remains the same; you simply change the details of who you're sending it to, and the title of the position you are applying for. So, if you are careful, Mr Bloggs from Platinum Ltd WILL receive a letter addressed to him, with the position he advertised.

If you're not careful, Mr Bloggs might receive a letter with a position that does not exist in his company because someone forgot to change the title of the position after sending a letter to Mr Farringdon in another company!

✔ **Specific' cover letter:** This format requires more modifications than the salutations. Always make sure to read the requirements of a cover letter in the original advertisement so you may respond accordingly. If the advert simply asks for 'a cover letter', use the general one as outlined above. If the advert asks that you reveal your present salary, do not start protesting in your mind about confidentiality. Employers try to use this as a bargaining tool from the offset. If you're on a salary that is less than the employer would offer, there is scope for them to offer you a marginally higher one. (For more on this strategy, see Chapter 6.)

A specific cover letter becomes more complicated when the employer asks you to state the reason you're applying for the position. Don't waffle about how you want to fulfil your dreams of corporate success or pine that you need the job because you have bills to pay. Simply let the employer know that you seek the appointment because you wish to use the skills you have acquired to enhance your career.

The employer is more likely to ask about your salary expectations in a specific cover letter. Remember to research the going rate for that position and submit a figure that does not under- or over-sell you.

Regardless of the type of letter you're writing, you need to make sure certain elements are covered. Including these elements will make the difference between being short-listed and your application ending up in the dustbin.

Always:

✔ Include your own address/contact details at the top of the letter.

✔ Write the formal details of the employer – never shorten first names.

✔ Use crisp, concise language, even though you write in the first person.

✔ Print your letter, unless the employer requested that you handwrite the document.

✔ Contain the letter on one A4 sheet of paper.

Also remember to use the correct salutations. (See the 'Closing salutations' section, later in this chapter.)

Writing the Cover Letter

You should write your cover letter after you've compiled your CV because by then, you've caught on to a style of writing that you believe will work and want to reflect this in the letter. (If you haven't created your CV, see Chapter 5.)

When you look over your final CV, concentrate on extracting information from the first page, specifically your Key Skills section and the current or most recent career summary details.

Your personal details must appear as they do at the top of your CV. You may want to cut and paste information into the top of the cover letter draft as you begin.

Employers won't scrutinise whether you range your information right or left, providing that the rest of the letter is laid out consistently. So, if you range your details to the right at the top of the page, make sure your closing salutations are in the same position and so forth. Remember to put the date beneath these details.

Opening salutations

Make sure you get the correct details of the person you're addressing the letter to. Advertisements always carry specific details as to how to apply for jobs. Sometimes there is a vacancy reference number, which should be quoted after your opening salutations. If the advertisement specifies the person's name but you're unsure whether the name is female or male, simply write 'Sam Thorne'. If however, it is obviously a woman but you're unsure as to titles, simply write 'Ms Thorne'. Make sure you write the correct address, including the full postcode.

The opening paragraph is straightforward. State that you're applying for the vacancy, writing the title of the job as it appears in the advertisement.

If you're compiling a 'speculative letter', the only change to the document would be the first paragraph. 'Speculative' letters are used to target companies that have not advertised but are likely to have ongoing vacancies. These include large companies, retail outlets and diverse employers. The first rule of speculating is to research the most appropriate companies you wish to target, and submit the 'speculative' letter in the hope they may call you for an interview.

The first paragraph of a cover letter is altered to read: 'I am enquiring whether there are current/future vacancies within the above company.' The rest of the letter can remain the same.

The body

At all times, remember that the cover letter is for you to say what you can bring to the job being advertised and why you want it. And the cover letter must be presented on one page. So, there is a need to restrict long sentences, excessive personal information, and a reiteration of the entire CV that you've already supplied.

The second and third paragraphs must include details of your current/most recent job or two most recent jobs. You can open with a sweeping statement to testify your skills in the field: 'I have a solid background in administration, executive and project assistance.' Try to amend it a little so that it does not copy word for word from your CV. After this, you summarise your remits at your present or most current employers.

Essentially, these paragraphs are used to sell your skills. Again, view your finished CV, particularly the two most recent jobs you've had. Summarise from the details of each appointment, highlighting the key remits. Remember that you may write in the first person in the cover letter, as against the style adopted in the CV.

This does not give you the licence to 'waffle' without fine-tuning the document. Remember to state your current job title and the number of years/months you've spent in that position. 'At the moment, I am appointed as Front House Concierge at the Olympia Hotel in London.' Use about three further sentences to describe your main duties.

Then skip a paragraph and compile the second paragraph, depicting the job you had before, using the same style/writing as on your CV document.

The next paragraph can mention the personal skills you've amassed in your employment. In this section, you may also state reasons you believe that you're suitable for the job. Unless there is a requirement for particular skills, such as fluency in languages, general statements can be made.

You can enhance the letter by alluding to special skills. For example, if the employer says he wants an 'effective negotiator', you can say you were involved in securing cost-effective products at your last job. But remember that you mustn't repeat information you've already put into the body of the letter.

Closing salutations

Follow conventions in this section. If the person is named in your opening salutation, you end the letter with 'Yours sincerely'. If a position has been stated, such as 'Head of Personnel Department', you end with 'Yours faithfully'.

Checking Out Cover Letter Examples

After you've crafted your letter and proofread it, you're ready to push the Upload command or the print button, and work your magic! Figures 11-1, 11-2 and 11-3 are examples of great cover letters that get it right.

3/1, Max Avenue
Glasgow, 00 00
Tel: 000 000
Email: recentgraduate@hotmail.com

Mr Richard Whyte
Head of Human Resources
CasaNova Plc., Queens Gate
London 00 00

Dear Mr Whyte

I apply for the position of <u>Sub-Stockbroker</u>, as advertised, in the Daily Times today.

I recently achieved a Master of Science degree in Corporate Finance and Investment from the London Metropolitan University. Prior to that, I completed a Graduate Certificate in Business. Sound academic skills are compounded by first-rate analytical skills to assimilate complex data and create effective solutions.

I have nurtured an avid interest in investment banking from an early age and seek the opportunity to develop substantial skills for long-term aspirations within the profession.

I have chosen to apply to CasaNova because the bank has an enviable international reputation for excellence in full-function services and recruits high-calibre graduates.

I have some experience in client relations, having been appointed Administrator at the Kane University of Science and Technology. I was responsible for managing daily workload within a demanding environment, implementing quality assurance policies and ensuring efficiency at all times. I liaised extensively with external partner organisations, establishing effective working relations and being integral in formulating client relations.

I am highly resilient, tenacious and committed to excellence in both professional and personal spheres. Please find enclosed, a copy of my Curriculum Vitae for your perusal. I look forward to your response at your earliest convenience.

Thank you.

Yours sincerely,

Recent Graduate

Figure 11-1: A cover letter from a recent graduate.

37 Millbank Drive
Berkshire, GU00 00
Home: 00 0 22333
Mobile: 0700 00000
E-mail: john_presley@hotmail.com
July 10, 2008

Mr Richard Whyte
Head of Human Resources
LearnDirect, Queens Gate
London 00 00

Dear Mr Whyte

I apply for the position of <u>Tutor - Business Studies</u>, as advertised in the 'Sunday Times' recently.

I have solid experience in tertiary and secondary education, with ability to design teaching material and raise levels of achievement amongst under-graduates and A' Level students. This is compounded by academic accolades, including a Master of Business Administration degree.

At the moment, I undertake remits as a private tutor for diverse clients in Berkshire. I deliver lessons to students pursuing A' Level Economics and related business subjects, liaising with parents as to their progress and monitoring general progress.

Between 1998 and 2006, I was assigned as a lecturer to various renowned educational institutions, including the University of East London. I taught Economics, Principles of Management, Human Resources Management, Organizational Behaviour and Marketing. I also undertook comprehensive management of course delivery, preparing teaching material, setting/marking examination scripts and supervising students' research projects. I exceeded 90% target passes for A' Level Economics.

I am highly resilient, tenacious and committed to quality standards in both professional and personal spheres. I also possess excellent interpersonal skills to become integral to achieving business objectives of the company. I seek an opportunity to utilise substantial transferable skills in Education and develop new ones. My strong background in strategic and general management will also be an asset to the company.

Please find enclosed, a copy of my Curriculum Vitae for your perusal. I look forward to your response at your earliest convenience. Thank you.

Yours sincerely

John Presley

Figure 11-2: A cover letter from a lecturer.

The King's Way
Norway
Tel: 004700 000 00 24
Email: atabyplace@yahoo.com

October 5, 2008

My Richard Whyte
Head of Human Resources
ICI Plc., Queens Gate
London 00 00

Dear Mr Whyte

I apply for the position of <u>HEAD OF OPERATIONS AND SCHEDULE MANAGEMENT</u>, as advertised in the 'Sunday Times' recently.

I have solid experience in senior management within diverse environments, with the ability to initiate and implement successful large-scale business development strategies and procure lucrative partnerships. This is compounded by first-rate analytical skills to formulate change management procedures and create effective solutions.

At the moment, I am appointed Manager of the Power Recovery Unit at ELKEM in Norway. I undertake comprehensive management of cross-functional projects from conception through to evaluation. Achievements to date include new design of boilers and filters, delivery of waste heat to the local community and development of energy-efficient work processes and system tools. As an integral member of the Executive Board, I implement sound quality assurance policies, collaborating with relevant stakeholders and external agencies to oversee international venture.

Prior to this, I acquired more than 18 years' experience in business management, including strategic and review programmes, and all functions from operations through to logistics and finance. I have spearheaded corporations with sales in excess of SEK 250 million, contributed to expansion over two years and worked in conjunction with interdisciplinary engineers.

I welcome the opportunity to work for a European market leader for renewable energy with a global reputation for excellence in service delivery. I wish to utilise substantial skills I have amassed and consolidate senior managerial skills in such a challenging environment. Please find attached, a copy of my Curriculum Vitae for your perusal.

I look forward to your response at your earliest convenience.

Yours sincerely

Andrew Regina

Figure 11-3: A cover letter from a senior manager

Part III
Bringing It All Together: Sample Targeted CVs

'It happens every time I start on my CV'

In this part . . .

You find sample CVs that show you what your targeted CV needs to look like to really pack a punch. We also explain ways of targeting different jobs with the same CV contents.

Chapter 12

Targeted CVs by Industry and Career Field

● ●

In This Chapter

▶ Keeping your eye on computers or people

▶ Finding a career in medicine

▶ Earmarking an engineering job

● ●

*N*o skeletons in your work history? No problems? If you're perfect, this is your kind of chapter. The sample CVs here reflect a range of CV formats for several industries, presented for maximum effect.

Targeted CV for IT or Management

When writing a CV for IT and related managerial positions, don't clutter the document with technical jargon. Remember that the employer knows the terminology you're used to, so minimise long-winded descriptions. See Figure 12-1 for an example of a CV targeted for IT or management positions.

TARGETED CV FOR IT/ MANAGEMENT

BILL YATES
0000000
Tel: 0000
Email: 0000000

SKILLS PROFILE

Experienced as Solutions Architect in business/technology development
Ability to manage multi-tasked teams and acheve significant results
Excellent interpersonal and negotiating skills to forge corporate relations

KEY ACHIEVEMENTS

Created and established thriving offshore development team in Qatar
Spearheaded major projects and teams of offshore developers in Russia

PROFESSIONAL/CAREER

Aug 2006-Date	**Diamond Qatar Company** General Manager Manage daily operational activities within a demanding environment. Supervise cross-functional staff teams. Develop business strategies, forging relations with diverse international corporations. Implement change projects, support pre- and post-sales in Canada and Sudan.
Oct 1999- **Aug 2006**	**Ruby Ltd., Huddersfield** IT Consultant and Project Manager Spearheaded entire development workload, providing technical support and ensuring quality standards. Investigated requirements, delivering presentations to identify and instigate solutions. Oversaw methodologies, products and projects at various stages of the lifecycle, collaborating with internal and external agents. Also devised and facilitated training programmes for end-users whilst implementing performance management.
Nov 1998- **Oct 1999**	**PTL (MCI-Worldcom), London** Software Developer Developed ad hoc software solutions in classic ASP, Visual Basic & SQL Server and VBA, for MCI-WorldCom.

Figure 12-1: Targeted CV for IT/Management

PROFESSIONAL/QUALIFICATIONS

1993-1997   **Kingston University**
                       Bachelor of Science (Hons 2:2)
                       - Applied Computing

Technical skills:

Visual Basic for ACCESS
SQL Server; Visual Basic
Crystal Reports; PHP & MySQL
Classic ASP 3 to 5 years

Figure 12-1 *(continued)*

Targeted CV for Medicine

Medical professionals highlight particular details in CVs to demonstrate skills in diverse clinical and management remits.

For example, elaborate on your teaching and auditing experience, or the types of procedures or training you've undertaken throughout your career. Always state your registration number with the General Medical Council UK or membership of other international bodies. Figure 12-2 shows an example of this type of CV.

TARGETED CV FOR MEDICINE

Dr GUSTAFO
00000 0000000
Tel: 0000000000000
Mobile: 000000000000
E-mail: 000000@000000000

GMC Reg: 0000000 (UK)
Member of British Medical Association
Member of Medical Defence Union

PROFESSIONAL/QUALIFICATIONS

2004	**Royal College of Physicians** Member - Royal College of Physicians
1997	**The Place University** Medical Doctor
1994	**South Pole University** MBBS

PROFESSIONAL/CAREER

Aug 2007-Aug 2008	**Resting Place Hospital** General Practice Registrar (GP ST3) Primary care management of acute and chronic cases with holistic approach. Integrated primary care within local hospital attached to the practice, comprising 20 beds. Undertake National Health Service (NHS) 24 Out Of Hours shifts allocated to the registrar year.
Feb - July 2007	**Second Resting Place Hospital** Senior House Officer (GPVTS) Obstetrics & Gynaecology Facilitated gynaecology in-hospital out-patients clinics and clinics during outreach programme. Integral to management of in-ward obstetrics & gynaecology patients, normal & assisted deliveries and operations such as LSCS, hysterectomy, etc.
Aug 2006 - Feb 2007	**The Place Hospital** Senior House Officer, Paediatrics Managed acutely ill cases in the ward, attended outpatients' clinics and assisted resuscitation.

Figure 12-2: Targeted CV for medicine.

Feb - Aug 2005	**The Second Place Hospital** Senior Clinical Fellow, Acute Medicine Performed assessment of acutely ill medical patients admitted to Medical Assessment Unit.
Aug 2004 - Feb 2005	**South East Hospital** Trust Grade Registrar Managed short stay patients, planned admissions/discharges, liaising with interdisciplinary teams comprising bed crisis staff, psychiatry services, occupational therapists and social services.
Jan 1999 - Feb 2004	**South West Hospital** (500-bed tertiary care centre serving as a referral hospital for the entire southwest region.)
(2002 - 2004)	Chief Medical Resident Medical Resident Responsible for patients in the medical ward and managed emergencies. Independently performed procedures such as central lines and temporary transvenous pacing.

FORMAL COURSES

Theoretical Course – Feb-March 2004
ILS (Intermediate Life Support) – May 2004
EPLS (European Paediatric Life Support) – July 2007
NRP (Neonatal Resuscitation Programme) Provider – August 2007
DFFP + STIF (Diploma Faculty of Family Planning & Sexually
Transmitted Infections)

TEACHING/ADMINISTRATION

Prepared monthly duty rotas, arranged cover duties for absent junior
doctors.
Implemented efficient administrative procedures (1994-2004).

Figure 12-2 *(continued)*

Targeted CV for Engineering

In some CVs, technical jargon is unavoidable because the industry is so specialist. This is evident in some types of engineering or scientific CVs, as shown in Figure 12-3.

TARGETED CV FOR NUCLEAR ENGINEERING

LOUIS BROWN
000000 000000
Tel: 0000000000000
Email: 0000000000

Date of Birth: 10 July 1968

KEY SKILLS

Experienced in operational management within the nuclear and related industries
Ability to initiate/implement large-scale health/safety and compliance projects
Excellent interpersonal and negotiating skills to forge partnerships with key stakeholders
Adapt well to challenges; resilient and tenacious

Associate Member of Institute of Chemical Engineering
Member of Ichem

PROFESSIONAL/CAREER

2004-Date   Head of Operating Unit, Chemflow
(Unit comprises facility for safe receipt, storage and decanning/dismantling of spent nuclear fuel; solvent extraction plant for the separation of uranium and plutonium and safe storage of plutonium and uranium products.)

Initiate/develop strategic objectives and quality standards. Manage maintenance of four nuclear reactors.

High volume of liaison with key regulators such as Health/Safety Executive and Department of Trade and Industry on operational issues. Represent Sellafield Ltd on stakeholder committees.

2004-2007   Head of Manufacturing, FutureCom
(Mechanical handling plant and associated effluent treatment facility for receipt, storage and decanning/dismantling of irradiated nuclear fuel from UK customers.)

Responsible for safe and efficient operation of plants covering 24-hour schedules. Controlled 16 million-pound budget. Oversaw 250 multi-tasked staff, implementing performance processes, ensuring compliance with safety and risk assessment standards.

Chair of the plant's Management Safety Committee, instigating change and safety management policies with the view to improving delivery and gaining endorsements.

Figure 12-3: Targeted CV for Engineering.

2002-2004   Head of Manufacturing, SafeTek
(Comprising solvent extraction plant combined with uranium and plutonium finishing plants and associated product stores.)

Similar managerial remits as aforementioned. Spearheaded six Independent Compliance Advisors, formulating strict health/safety regulations. Facilitated advisory sessions to operating units on adherence to policies.

1995-2000   Manufacturing Support Manager, Graves Plants
Integral member of team comprising 20 professional engineers and scientists providing troubleshooting and safety case management service.

Implemented safety assessment (including HAZOP/HAZAN). Interpreted output of safety assessments into clear plant instructions for accurate compliance. Collaborated with safety regulators such as HSE and Nuclear Installations Inspectorate, reviewing safety cases and executing appropriate change procedures.

PROFESSIONAL/QUALIFICATIONS

1983   Leeds University
Bachelor of Science (Hons 2:1) -
Chemical Engineering

Figure 12-3 *(continued)*

Chapter 13

Targeted CVs by Experience Level and Age

. . . .

In This Chapter

▶ Creating a CV when you have no experience

▶ Matching your experience level to the job

. . . .

Do you have reason to think that you have too much experience – or not enough – to rack up the job offers you want? Or that you're too young – or too old? The sample CVs in this chapter show techniques aimed at downplaying negative perceptions about your experience or your age.

School-Leaver with No Work Experience

If you're a school-leaver, you're unlikely to have had substantial work experience because of restrictions on getting paid employment before you turn 16. However, you can still enhance your CV, as Figure 13-1 shows.

If you did work experience in Year 11 at an organisation, shop or office, put this information on your CV. Include any extracurricular activities such as sport, debates or fund-raising days.

Graduate with Some Experience

If you have more than two years' commercial experience in the profession you graduated in, start your CV with these details. If you have experience in other stop-gap areas, start your CV with your qualifications and state your work experience afterwards, as shown in Figure 13-2.

Management CV

As a manager climbing the corporate ladder, each rung indicates you're acquiring more applicable skills for long-term aspirations. If you have more than eight years' experience in management, you may want to include your professional achievements on your CV. See an example of this in Figure 13-3.

Senior Executive CV

Having more than 15 years' experience in any industry is cause for celebration, especially if you aspire to become a senior partner or associate of the company. This type of format differs from a management CV because it highlights overall achievements at the top of the CV to catch the employer's eyes straightaway, as shown in Figure 13-4. You may, at your discretion, put further details for each position.

SCHOOL-LEAVER - NO WORK EXPERIENCE

DEMI ADECHIE
000 000, London
S00 000
Tel: 0000000000

EDUCATION/TRAINING

2004–Date   Ridge Academy
               Pursuing GCSE subjects:
               Mathematics; English; Science (Double Award); ICT; Art and Graphic Arts

WORK EXPERIENCE

To Date   Babysitter
               Attend to younger children, taking them from school and assisting with
               homework. Also assist them with practical tasks such as meals.

INTERESTS

Computer games, socializing and theatre

Figure 13-1: A CV for a school-leaver with no work experience.

GRADUATE WITH SOME EXPERIENCE

JANE OSBORNE
000000000
0000000000000
Tel: 000000
Email: 00000

SKILLS PROFILE

Sound experience in silkscreen printing in diverse settings
Ability to work on own initiative under pressure and to deadlines
Ability to motivate multi-tasked teams and achieve results
Excellent interpersonal/negotiating skills to forge partnerships
Adapt well to challenges; resilient and tenacious

Relevant experience:

Hand bench screenprinting (created A1 Underground posters)
Prepare stencils for printing, photograph and electronic methods
Utilise exposure unit, setting up a manual press and maintain efficient prints

PROFESSIONAL/QUALIFICATIONS

2006-2009	**London Central University**
	Bachelor of Arts - (Hons 2:1) - Fine Art Invaluable practical insight into screenprinting, woodcut, collograph and lino printing techniques. Enhanced skills in creative writing, research and planning.
2000-2003	**Lottie College**
	AVCE Art and Design (Grade AA)
1995-2000	**Seaview High School**
	GCSE subjects (Grades B-D) Including English, Art, Mathematics and Information Technology

EMPLOYMENT SUMMARY

2005-Date	**Greggs Bakery**
	General Assistant
	High volume of customer relations, issuing information about varied products, processing payment transactions and handling general queries. Carried out price and stock control, coordinating delivery schedules and liaising with suppliers.

Figure 13-2: A CV for a graduate with some experience.

Work within multi-tasked teams of 10
staff members, under pressure and to tight deadlines.

2001-2003   **Mr Loaf's Bakery**
                    <u>Sales Assistant</u>
                    Similar duties as above, processing
                    payments, reconciling cash and carrying out merchandising.

<u>**PERSONAL INFORMATION**</u>

Date of Birth: November 10, 1978

Interests:
Attending to animals, wildlife documentaries, foreign films and classical novels.

Pursuing evening course in the Russian language.

Figure 13-2 *(continued)*

MANAGEMENT CV

ALAN SALT
00000 000
000000000
Tel: 0000000000000
Email:

Solid experience in financial management in diverse settings
Practical knowledge of Microsoft Series/management software
Excellent interpersonal and negotiating skills to forge relations

PROFESSIONAL / CAREER

2000–2008	**The Lakeside Experience**
	Branch Manager

Spearheaded business development programmes, instigating strategic plan to maximise profitability. Orchestrated interdisciplinary staff members comprising customer relations, shop and support personnel. Implemented effective customer relations procedures, performance management and annual appraisal systems.

Other remits involved implementing cost-effective measures, negotiating with suppliers and other external agencies. High volume of liaison with senior management teams on business reviews.

Achievements:
Attained 100% on mystery shopper, working to KPI including sales, mystery shopper, stock loss and costs.
Recruited/developed highly motivated staff members.
Introduced self-training programmes for all functions.

Jan–Sept 2000	**The Sun Palace**
	Branch Manager

Initiated excellent customer relations management policies, formulating company's performance systems and Centre of Excellence within branch. Carried out financial control, instigating budgets and cost-effective systems. Staff management as aforementioned.

Achievements:
Introduced branch standards on stock display overflow.
Instrumental in setting up store infrastructure, successfully coordinating closure and re-launch to tight schedules.

1997-1999	**The Rain Place**
	Branch Manager

Figure 13-3: An example of a management CV.

Responsible for profitability of outlet, managing 12 multi-tasked staff members and monitoring KPIs. Assimilated market intelligence to determine competitiveness, implemented financial procedures and oversaw operational activities. Coordinated promotions, discount sales and charity fashion shows, liaising extensively with Head Office. Compiled detailed reviews and delivered presentations to senior management teams. Instigated
risk and health/safety processes.

Achievements:
Registered second highest profit margin of all outlets in the UK and Ireland (behind Oxford Street, London) in 1999.

PROFESSIONAL/QUALIFICATIONS

National College of Ireland/Western Management Institute.
Diploma in Business Management & Employee Relations
Customer Service; Training the Trainer;
Health & Safety at Work; Lateral Thinking;
Customer Complaint Handing; Retail Selling Skills
Supervisory in Approach to People; Handling Crisis Situations

Figure 13-3 *(continued)*

SENIOR EXECUTIVE CV

MR LEYLAND
000000000000000
0000000000000
00000000

SKILLS SUMMARY

Experienced in global logistics management and related roles
Ability to initiate/implement strategic and change management
Strong analytical skills to assimilate data and create solutions
Practical knowledge of associated haulage/freight software

KEY ACHIEVEMENTS

Procured key contract, third-largest global corporation
Created logistics company to register 1.4 million+ turnover
Established enviable international reputation for services

PROFESSIONAL/CAREER

2004-Date   Mr Leyland Company
                        General Manager
                                Undertake comprehensive management of
                                multi-million full-function global logistics
                                company. Initiate strategic account and
                                business planning, achieving Key Performance
                                Indicators and quality assurance policies.

                                Spearhead commercial and budgetary units, monitoring cost
                                control and added value
                                services. Collaborate with key contractual
                                partnerships primarily throughout EMEA
                                regions and worldwide. Sole responsibility
                                for developing new business and procuring
                                lucrative contracts.

                                Formulate effective performance procedures,
                                identify and facilitate appropriate training programmes to
                                enhance productivity. Implement health/safety and risk
                                assessment polices and ensure compliance
                                with statutory and company policies.

                                Achievements:
                                Established company to 1.4 million-pound
                                turnaround in less than four years.
                                Recruited/selected collaborative staff.
                                Recently attained ISO 2000 accreditation.

Figure 13-4: A CV for a senior executive.

1994-2004	Thorough Freight Services
	<u>Operations Manager</u>

Similar managerial remits as aforementioned. Also coordinated teams with more than 43 staff members, implementing concrete performance management policies and ensuring efficiency at all times.

Involved in review/change management processes to achieve business objectives. Assimilated market intelligence to determine performance and devised alternative strategies to combat competition. Forged relations with numerous external agencies, working in conjunction with Finance, Sales and Marketing departments.

PROFESSIONAL/EDUCATION

CPC National and International Freight
Occupational Health & Safely/ISOH
Health and Safety within the Workplace
First Aid in the Workplace
Forklift Licence
European Computer Driving Licence
A+ Computer Hardware; Software; Networking
Five GCSE O'Level subjects including mathematics and English

ADDITIONAL INFORMATION

I have in-depth knowledge of European and worldwide business and cultural diversity, having lived for seven years in South Africa and travelled extensively throughout the world. At the moment, I am delegate to the District Police Partnership and Training Coordinator for a local Judo Club.

Date of Birth: August 2, 1962
<u>Interests:</u> Fitness training, networking and family life

REFERENCES AVAILABLE UPON REQUEST

Figure 13-4 *(continued)*

Chapter 14

Targeted CVs for Special Circumstances

• •

In This Chapter

▶ Finding a job in the education field

▶ Changing your CV to match different fields

• •

*W*hether you're changing your career from being a stockbroker to becoming a teacher, or switching directions because you need new challenges in new environments, you can create a riveting CV. The samples in this chapter give you some ideas about how to do just that by deftly handling your special circumstances.

Changing a Qualified Teacher's CV for Jobs in Education and Management

Targeting your CV from one industry to another is effective if you follow guidelines. Firstly, you highlight your skills that are relevant to the position you seek, then you elaborate on all skills you assume might be useful, as Figure 14-1 shows.

Likewise, this applicant can use the same CV and recast it to target management positions, as can be seen in Figure 14-1.

QUALIFIED TEACHER TARGETING JOBS IN EDUCATION

GARY TRIM
00000000000000000
0000000000000000
00000000000

Master of Business Administration
Solid experience in tertiary and secondary education
Extensive background in strategic and business management
Ability to supervise teaching teams and achieve results

PROFESSIONAL/CAREER
(Relevant)

2006-Date	**Private Tutor** Devise/deliver lessons to students pursuing GCSE and A'Level Economics and related business subjects. Liaise with parents as to student progress.
1998-2006	Various Secondary Schools **Lecturer** Assigned to renowned educational institutes. Marked examination scripts and supervised students' research projects. Maintained records of students' attendance. Disseminated information to A' Level students relating to university transition and employability issues.

(Other)

2001-Date	The Guards **Security Officer** Provide security services to diverse corporate clients across 16 sites throughout Surrey. Confident Debt Recovery **Telesales Agent** High volume of public liaison, securing sales for homecare products on behalf of British Gas and Southern Electric.
2001-2006	Guardian Life Insurance **Sales Representative** Processed wide range of policies, qualifying private clients for life insurance. Underwrote relevant documentation and provided aftercare services.
1989-2001	Telephonics & Wireless **Manager/Supervisor**

Figure 14-1: A teacher's CV targeting jobs in education.

Spearheaded large-scale telecommunications projects, liaising extensively with government, public and private sector agencies.

PROFESSIONAL/QUALIFICATIONS

1996-1998	Nova Scotia University MBA
1994-1996	Nova Scotia University Bachelor in Professional Management
1988-1989	University of Leeds Certificate in Business Administration
1997	Institute of Management Certificate in Purchasing & Inventory Control

Figure 14-1: *(continued)*

FOR MANAGEMENT POSITIONS

GARY TRIM
00000000000000000
0000000000000000
00000000000

KEY SKILLS

Master of Business Administration
Extensive background in strategic and business management
Ability to supervise teams and achieve significant results
Excellent interpersonal and negotiating skills to forge relations

PROFESSIONAL/CAREER

(Relevant)

2006 - Date	Private Tutor	Devise/deliver lessons to students pursuing GCSE A'Level Economics and related business subjects. Liaise with parents as to students' progress and draft individual programmes to raise levels of achievement.
2001-Date	**Confident Debt Recovery** Administrative Associate	Issued advice on mortgage and debt recovery process.
2001-2006	**Guardian Life Insurance** Sales Representative	Qualified/underwrote private clients for life insurance.
1989-2001	**Telephonics and Wireless** Manager/Supervisor	Integral member of management team establishing new external construction unit. Spearheaded large-scale projects, instigating due diligence. Oversaw 52 staff members. Controlled budgets/logistics.

PROFESSIONAL/QUALIFICATIONS

1996-1998	**Nova Scotia University** MBA
1994-1996	**Nova Scotia University** Bachelor in Professional Management
1988-1989	**University of Leeds** Certificate in Business Administration
1997	**Institute of Management** Certificate in Purchasing & Inventory Control

Figure 14-2: A teacher's CV targeting jobs in management.

Creating Specialist CVs

Some CVs don't follow the conventional style with two pages, names of employers, job titles, duties and so on. Some professions are more interested in a candidate's track record and don't deliberate on how wonderful the candidate may be in analysing data or controlling budgets. The facts speak for themselves in specialist CVs.

In Figure 14-3, Elmi Abdul tailors his CV to nab a job as an architect.

ELMI ABDUL - PROJECTS AND COMPANIES

Project Date	Company	Project Specifications
2003-to date	THE HILTON GROUP LTD & CUCINA INTERIORS, LONDON (Project procurement, management & consultancy)	- Templars - Private Residence for Sheikh in his family's private estate on River Thames. Estimated budget for new project £2.5 million. - Chancery Lane, Pimlico. Private residence in beautiful setting. - The Dock Harbour, London SW10. Investment apartment with River Thames views. - Interior design coordination/procurement of interior finishes from Italy for private apartments at Panton Square, Mayfair W1, Cherry Gardens Chelsea, Mount Pleasant Mayfair. Budgets ranging from £100K-£250K.
Sept 1999-to Oct 2003	RELIANCE INTERIORS (Building & construction management. Interior design coordinators)	- Treasure Garden, London EC. Residential development of new build 17 flats for Park Lane Properties, London. Project value £2.5 million.

Figure 14-3: An architect's specialist CV.

Targeting Community Sector and Medical Positions

Figure 14-4 shows how a medical doctor can apply for a position in community sector organisations; in Figure 14-5 she targets medical positions.

CV TARGETING COMMUNITY SECTOR POSITIONS

MARTHA BRAE
00 00000000000000
Tel: 00000000000
E-mail: 00000

PROFESSIONAL/BACKGROUND

(Relevant Career)

2007-Date	Health and Family Services Trustee Integral to management of community sector organisation providing diverse health education and advisory services to women in Tower Hamlets.
2007-Date	The Sickle Cell & Thalassemia Centre Community Development Worker High volume of liaison with interdisciplinary teams, instigating quality assurance policies and devising outreach programmes into community settings.
2001-2007	Voluntary Counsellor
2007-Date	Action for Health Advisory Group Member Collaborating with professional counterparts, including hospital consultants, NHS Professionals, PCT representatives and community health advisors.
2007-Date	Area Action Plan Consultation Group Advisory Group Member Similar remits as aforementioned.
2004-Date	The Community Project, New Cross Lecturer

(Career in Medicine)

2005-2006	St Augustos NHS Trust Clinical Fellow (SHO Level) in Obstetrics & Gynaecology with special interest in urogynaecology.
2004-2005	Uxbridge Hospital NHS Trust Senior House Officer - Obstetrics and Gynaecology
2003-2004	Peter's NHS Trust; Weston NHS Trust Senior House Officer - Obstetrics and Gynaecology

Figure 14-4: A CV targeting community sector jobs.

2002-2003   The Central NHS Trust
                  Locum Senior House Officer Honorary Observer

PROFESSIONAL/QUALIFICATIONS

2006-Date   King George College
                  Pursuing Master of Science - Public Health

1996   MBBS

Have completed the following professional courses:

2008   Mental Health NHS Trust
                  Mental Well-being Impact Assessment Training

                  Women's Resource Centre
                  Using Public Law and Gender Duty
                  Budgeting and Financial Planning

                  Domestic Violence, Immigration Law and No recourse to Public Funds

ADDITIONAL INFORMATION
I am a member of the Fine Women London/City Gateway consultation group.
Date of Birth: August 20, 1975

REFERENCES AVAILABLE UPON REQUEST

Figure 14-4: *(continued)*

Here, in Figure 14-5, Martha's CV has been revised so that it targets medical positions.

CV TARGETING MEDICINE

MARTHA BRAE
00 00000000000000
Tel: 00000000000
E-mail: 00000

PROFESSIONAL/BACKGROUND

(Relevant Career)

2005-2006	St Augustos NHS Trust Clinical Fellow (SHO Level) Obstetrics & Gynaecology with special interest in urogynaecology.	
2004-2005	Uxbridge Hospital NHS Trust Senior House Officer - Obstetrics and Gynaecology	
2003-2004 2003-2005	Peter's NHS Trust; Weston NHS Trust Senior House Officer - Obstetrics and Gynaecology	
2002-2003	The Central NHS Trust Locum Senior House Officer Honorary Observer	
2007-Date	Health and Family Services Trustee Integral to management of community sector organisation providing diverse health education and advisory services to women in Tower Hamlets.	
2007-Date	The Sickle Cell & Thalassemia Centre Community Development Worker High volume of liaison with interdisciplinary teams, instigating quality assurance policies and devising outreach into community settings.	
2001-2007	Voluntary Counsellor	
2007-Date	Action for Health Advisory Group Member Collaborating with professional counterparts, including hospital consultants, NHS Professionals, PCT representatives and community health advisors.	
2007-Date	Area Action Plan Consultation Group Advisory Group Member Similar remits as aforementioned.	

Figure 14-5: This time, the CV targets medical positions.

| 2004-Date | The Community Project, New Cross |
| | Lecturer |

PROFESSIONAL/QUALIFICATIONS

| 2006-Date | King George College |
| | Pursuing Master of Science - Public Health |

| 1996 | MBBS |

CLINICAL EXPERIENCE

Manage Obstetric and Gynaecological emergencies, common gynaecological problems; Major/minor surgical procedures; Care of pregnant women in antenatal/post-natal; Daily patient care in the ward and clinic.

Identify common genito-urinary problems and psycho-social complaints; Neonatal resuscitation; Hypertension; Diabetes; Pulmonary embolism; DVT and acute infections; Special skills with mentally ill patients; Clinical sessions in Outpatient and community visits during training period; Adult and paediatric patient group.

Overseas:
Six months in Medicine, six months in Obstetrics & Gynaecology with rotation in Accident & Emergency Department; PRHO in Medicine; Three months in General Medicine and remaining in Paediatrics, Psychiatry and other branches of medicine; Undertook full-time with oncall 1 in 5.

Venepuncture; Cannulations; Blood transfusion; Lumbar punctures; Bone marrow aspirations; Pleural and peritoneal fluid aspirations; Resuscitation of patients in casualty.

AUDITING

CNS Abnormality detected prenatally - the outcome and follow up SHO Obs & Gynae (Royal London Hospital).
Audit of fast track referral system for Pelvic Masses – to assess compliance to the standards set out for assessing the patients with pelvic masses (COG Guideline) (SHO Obs & Gynae, Weston General Hospital).

ADDITIONAL INFORMATION
I am a member of the Fine Women London/City Gateway consultation group, which procures funding to provide diverse programmes to residents of Tower Hamlets.

Date of Birth: August 20, 1975

REFERENCES AVAILABLE UPON REQUEST

Figure 14-5: *(continued)*

Part IV
Launching Your CV Into Orbit

'Well, for a start, it's your spelling.....'

In this part . . .

You find tips and tricks to ensure your CV works its hardest when you send it to potential employers. We explain how to get the best references, increase your chances of getting an interview and acing the interview when you're there.

Chapter 15

References Authenticate Your CV

In This Chapter

▶ Acknowledging the harm of a lacklustre reference

▶ Choosing your referees while keeping your job search quiet

▶ Managing references to back up claims on your CV

*A*nd just like that, the job offer goes missing. You thought you had this one in the bag. Chances are, if the job itself wasn't cancelled or a background check didn't knock you out of the offer, you can blame your references for shooting you down.

Although verifiable statistics are elusive, we've come across several startling small-scale reference-checking surveys. The surveys assert that 50 to 64 per cent of all referees rate their subjects as mediocre to poor! Upon reflection, we think the assessment could well be true. That's because the management of references is the last frontier to be recognised as an activity vital to promising career development.

The Harm Caused by a So-So Reference

A reference doesn't have to be a broadside to sink your ship. A few of the many subtle ways to wreck your chances include such seemingly innocuous comments from referees as these:

> ✔ *Oh, is she still working in this field?*
>
> ✔ *He gave my name as a reference?*
>
> ✔ *I can't go into detail but she's not eligible for re-employment here.*
>
> ✔ (Long pause, followed by a disgusted tone of voice) *Oh yes; I do remember him.*

Sometimes referees use the avoidance dodge – they simply don't return calls asking about your performance. (Employers aren't legally required to provide references.)

A little foresight on your part can help ensure that your references aren't wrecking your search. References are power hitters in the hiring process because they provide validation of your claims to be a superior performer and candidate. (To find out exactly how to weed bad references out of your line-up, see the upcoming section 'Stamp out bad references'.)

We tend to view good references as entitlements, merely assuming they'll be there when we need them if we've done good work. Sorry, but that's yesteryear's thinking. Today's thinking is more like 'Trust, but verify.'

Seven Things You Need to Do about References

Managing your references – or reference management – is a key factor in managing your career. As a job-search tool, reference management seems to have soared to a new height during the past five years or so. There are several reasons: the globalisation of employment, a churning job market, and increasingly risk-adverse employers who want to be assured that they're making the right choices.

As you search for jobs, you may want to rethink references and to consider how they hurt your chances when they're negative, or modest, or even positive but not concretely connected to your aspirations. These pointers show you how to make sure others sing your praises.

Ban references from your CV

Create a second document with the names, correct telephone numbers, and addresses of referees. Supply this sheet only upon request. Don't burn out your referees by allowing too many casual callers access to their names and contact information. Employers typically don't spend the time and money to check references until after you're interviewed and are on the short list of potential employees.

Sending reference letters with a CV to recruiters isn't a good move. Recruiters are likely to assume the letters are either bogus or written by close friends. Including a reference letter with your initial submittal may make you seem desperate (and that's not good).

Expect employers to check references

In times gone by, employers didn't always bother to check references. The majority check now. Small employers still may not, but medium-sized and large companies, afraid of making an employment mistake, are taking aim on your past.

Rules vary from sector to sector and the type of employment. A significant number of employers request in-depth references. They normally send out a form for your previous or current employer to fill in, asking them various questions about you. Sometimes, employers request a Criminal Records Bureau check, especially when you may be working with vulnerable adults, young people and children.

When it's no secret that you're going to leave your current job, ask your company's human resources specialist what the exact company policy is for providing references. You may find it's essentially job title and employment verification dates, and perhaps salary confirmation and whether you're eligible for re-employment.

You may discover that your company is outsourcing reference information to private companies that charge a fee to prospective employers for your reference information. If that's your company's policy, try to get your work history in writing before you leave your job, which will save a prospective employer money, time and irritation.

Choose references with thought

List referees who have direct knowledge of your job performance. If necessary, go beyond your immediate supervisor and include past or present co-workers, subordinates, customers, suppliers, members of trade associations, or anyone else who can praise your work. Don't use relatives or friends for personal references; they have no direct knowledge of your performance in the job.

What's a good way to line up references? Skip this technique if you're doing a secret search, but if it's out in the open you can ask your boss whether he will give you a good reference. Ask for particulars regarding how your boss sees your accomplishments, competencies, skills, strengths and weaknesses. If your boss squirms and mumbles, you're probably a sitting duck for a less-than-glowing recommendation.

Checking out co-workers, you can say: 'Terry, I'm beginning a job search. Do you feel you know me well enough to provide a reference commenting on my skills in budget management?' If Terry declines, it's a blessing in disguise to find out before giving his name as a referee.

Never list a referee until you have that person's permission to do so.

Help references help you

Providing refereees with your CV is standard operating procedure. Go further: Write a short script of likely questions with a summary of persuasion points under each question.

In addition to general good words about your industriousness, creativity and leadership, focus on the industry. If you're applying to a financial institution, suggest that your references dwell on trustworthiness, conservatism and good judgement. If you're applying at a high-tech company that has proprietary software and inventions, ask your referees to stress your ethics and loyalty.

Send a brief email to referees identifying the qualifications you highlighted when you customised your CV for a given position (see Chapter 1). Say: 'I hope you can work that qualification in if you have an opening.'

Although you don't want to wear out your welcome and become a pest, try to keep in touch with your referees. Let them know how you're doing. Take them out to coffee or lunch occasionally.

Play safe with a reference folder

A letter of recommendation isn't particularly effective, but it is better than nothing in cases where a company disappears, your boss dies, or the referee is difficult to reach. Begin now to collect praise in a reference folder, also called a *reference dossier.* Routinely arrange for a reference letter when you leave a job, as well as copies of your appraisals, and place them in the folder.

You can't assume referees will come up with the points and words you need, so you may have to draft the letters and statements yourself. Try to have each reference cover a different qualification with some overlap for emphasis. Tactfully offer to draft the letter to save your referee time.

What else goes in your reference folder? Include a page or two of endorsements – the quoted actual words of several referees. Each statement needs to be signed with the name, title and company of the referee. Use the endorsement sheets as follow-ups to your CV to gain an interview, or to leave behind as reminders at interviews.

Stamp out bad references

If you were axed or pressed to resign, or if you told your boss what you thought of him and resigned, move immediately to damage-control alertness. Even if you were cool enough to obtain a letter of reference before you left, you absolutely must try to neutralise the reference.

A script to neutralise a damaging reference

Katie worked 18 months at a small company, where she received consistently good write-ups from the owner, but was fired by Jenny, a supervisor who was jealous of Katie's positive relationship with the company owner. Katie's friend made some calls and verified that Jenny was lying to prospective employers and telling them that Katie didn't do her job and wasn't a good employee. What can Katie do to improve her reference from Jenny?

Katie needs to call Jenny, speaking in a very calm, non-threatening tone, saying that she understands a bad reference is being given and that the reference is closing doors to employment. Katie nicely, but firmly, tells Jenny that this has to stop.

If Jenny is unresponsive or won't come to the phone or return a voicemail – which is very likely – Katie needs to write a letter to Jenny with the same message and send a copy of it to the owner of the company. Katie doesn't have to threaten litigation in the letter because any business manager with common sense will read between the lines that Katie's next step is to sue.

Katie's goal is not a total reversal of the negative evaluation but to obtain a neutral (but not mediocre) reference from the ex-employer.

Additionally, Katie can call the owner and explain the situation, saying that she doesn't want to cause any problems but wants to be able to go to work. She needs to ask the owner to be the one to provide future references since he has first-hand knowledge of her work and she's only asking that he tell the truth. Katie can remind the owner that she had been at the company for a year and a half, had a good track record, good reviews, and until the particular run-in with Jenny, everything had been smooth. If she can't get the owner on the phone, the best option is to write him a letter saying the same thing. The last thing the owner of a small company wants is a lawsuit over an employment reference.

If every effort Katie makes fails, and she is dead certain of receiving another bad reference, she can say to interviewers: 'I do have excellent references with every previous employer. My last supervisor's personality was very difficult. I believe she will not give me a glowing reference. Others in the company will testify to my diligence and work ethic. I will provide those names and titles. So if you check references with my previous employer, please check *all* of the people I was associated with there.'

As a last resort, Katie can offer to work on a temporary basis for 90 days to prove herself – a willingness that, along with collateral good references, communicates a brand of commitment that's hard to resist.

Appeal to a sense of fair play or guilt. Sometimes just saying that you're sorry and that you hope that the employer won't keep you from earning a living will be enough. Sometimes it won't.

When you've tried and failed to overcome a bad reference, you have three options:

- ✔ Drown the poor reference in large numbers of favourable references.

- ✔ Find a lawyer who will write a letter threatening legal action for libel or slander to the person who is giving you a bad rap. This approach is surprisingly effective.

- ✔ Continue your job hunt, concentrating on small firms that may not check references or that may be more inclined to take a chance on someone.

Thank everyone

When your job search is finished, remember your manners: Thank the people who were willing to help you. Not only is it common courtesy but you never know when you may need them again.

Finding References without Shedding Your Cloak of Secrecy

You know that it's smart to snare a new job before giving up your current position. But the Catch-22 is that you can't give as references your boss or other managers at your current company or the cat will be out of the bag.

You have a couple of options for getting references while keeping your job search under wraps.

- ✔ Use the names of former supervisors at other companies, preferably people you've kept in touch with and tipped off in advance about your search, as well as reliable contacts from professional organisations.

Don't give the names of co-workers or current suppliers or vendors: You can't be sure they won't inadvertently let slip that you're on the market, or even purposely curry favour with your management by whispering in the boss's ear.

✔ Emphasise to prospective employers that your job search is confidential. When an offer looks imminent, say that when you receive a signed offer letter, you'll be pleased for the prospective employer to check with your current management and that if you don't stack up as expected, you understand the job offer is null and void.

Allow Enough Time for Skilful Reference Management

In this time-starved world, busy people may take longer than you expect to come to your aid in perfecting a quality reference. When the time between your request for a reference and the referee's response seems stretched beyond endurance, it helps to remember that you give the reference a much higher priority than does the referee. Allow yourself plenty of lead time to drum up reference deliveries. People who like you want to cheer you onward and upward, but it's a busy life.

Chapter 16

Following Up on Your CV

- -

In This Chapter

▶ Handling voicemail like a pro

▶ Asking the right questions before following up

▶ Adapting sales techniques that really work

▶ Applying the Follow-Up Matrix to best use your time

- -

*Y*ou submitted your CV describing how you qualify for a targeted position. It's a work of art! Or so you thought. Four weeks have passed and the silence is deafening. Except for an automated response of receipt, you've heard nothing. Doesn't anyone care? You do. The problem is, you care more than the employer does.

We know that, because we haven't heard from a single employer complaining about a lack of CVs. But the most-asked question we receive these days is this:

> *My online CVs have gone missing; what can I do about it?*

The quick answer, assuming you didn't set up your CV's journey with networking or employee referrals in advance (see Chapter 3), is to know the ropes of CV post-submission and to follow up in ways you never had to think about before. This chapter has you covered.

Follow-Up Efforts Are Essential

When employers and recruiters don't see the benefits of spending time talking with you, they become masters of the game of 'catch me if you can'. Even if you do manage to talk your way past assistants and get managers on the phone, they may be evasive, even brusque. Despite the risks of rude receptions, acquiring the art of following up for something you want can be one of the smartest things you ever do, for the following reasons:

- ✓ **Lightning strikes.** Sometimes a manager, who has been meaning to fill a position but has been too busy putting out fires, responds favourably to the candidate who happens to call on a day when he just has time to exhale. It's a bit of the luck of the draw.

- ✓ **Persistence produces.** Some employers wait to judge which candidates have the most follow-through by how well they follow up. This 'test' applies not only to sales but to other endeavours where a prized competence is the ability to 'stay on top of things'.

- ✓ **Control empowers.** By grasping and adapting the successful strategies crack sales professionals use to get an appointment, you dramatically reduce the amount of frustration, letdown, and low self-esteem you may be feeling because you're taking charge and doing everything you can.

The vast majority of employers – as many as eight out of ten who use applicant tracking systems (see Chapter 6) – send out an automatic response to your application. The response says you'll be contacted if you match a job opening.

The automatic response rate of independent recruiters is unclear, but if you're a potential candidate for a job opening they're trying to fill, a recruiter will call you fairly quickly; if not, you may get an auto-response or no response.

Not many employers write to confirm they've received your CV. If you're fortunate enough to receive a letter of confirmation, read the contents and follow instructions. If the employer states that she'll contact you within a specific time if you're short-listed, wait until the time has expired, then telephone to find out whether you made the list. If the employer says she'll only contact short-listed people within a certain time, when that time has passed, you can call for feedback on your application.

Questions to Ask Yourself Before Following Up

When you're uncertain about how to make employers and recruiters hear what you're saying and offer you an interview, plan your follow-up campaign in advance. These questions and answers can help you fill in the blanks.

Do I phone or email my follow-up?

CV blasting rarely gets interviews. Email pitches rarely get interviews. You may argue with that judgement, noting that you lose your nerve on the phone and don't come across as accomplished and confident and so you should stick with email. You think some 'shy' people just can't sell themselves by phone even if they can sell other things.

You may be right. Telemarketing yourself is tough stuff. So is getting yourself recognised on the Internet. You probably need help from others in overcoming 'telephonophobia'.

You can gather several jobless friends and practise on each other. Or go way out and take a temp job as a telemarketer to become somewhat desensitised to rejection after rejection. You may never become really comfortable pitching yourself, but at least you won't faint or fold when you're told to 'Get off this phone and never call me again!'

 The consensus of specialists in job search and sales is that human voices are more persuasive than email messages. Email can, however, pave the way for your phone call. You can address a recruitment officer and say:

> *My proven background in supply-chain management looks like a good fit for your advertised requirements and quali-fications for the assistant manager position. I'm unsure whether you're at the interview phase yet but I would be delighted to answer any preliminary questions you may have. I'll call you tomorrow at 9:30 a.m.*

What powerful opening statement can I make?

The most powerful message to launch your call is to immediately mention the name of someone who referred you,
someone who the hiring manager cares about. This may be a
company executive, company employee, client, fellow professional, family member and so on.

What are other compelling opening statements?

Your accomplishments and results in past jobs or endeavours are what give your pitch a critical edge. Here are several
examples:

> *In my current position, I led a team to develop new sales
> strategies which this year boosted each store's sales by
> £90,000 per month.*

> *I was vice president of the campus economics club – second
> in leadership of 45 members. Our competitive project, which
> I chaired, was rated the best in a national competition.*

> *When my employer's off-shore customer service experiment
> failed, the department was recalled to Lancaster. I put in
> place a new process to handle complaints that boosted cus-
> tomer satisfaction by 45 per cent.*

After making your opening statement with your accomplishments, follow with a request to meet face to face: 'If you're
interested in knowing more about that, can we fix a time when
I could come in for a short talk?'

How much information can I find out from a central phone operator?

If the company you're calling employs a central phone operator or receptionist, you may get lucky and find out the very
information you need from that individual to follow up on
your CV.

One road block: Companies sometimes impose an information freeze that forbids releasing the names of their employees. The companies train people who answer phones to conform to the no-loose-talk policy. (Read the next question for some ideas on how to counter an information freeze.)

In many offices, the central phone operator is a welcoming individual who's probably treated like a robot and will buy into an approach that recognises her inner human being. Be friendly, and then say something like this:

> *Please tell me, who is the manager for the new product marketing department? Oh thank you. I appreciate your help. And could you also tell me who the manager reports to? Thank you very much.*

If you're bonding with the central phone operator – you provide the only real conversation the operator has in a long day of fielding call after call – go for broke. Ask for the manager's secretary's name, the best time to call, how to pronounce the manager's name, and whether the manager works early, late or at weekends. Aim to uncover your target's direct telephone number – or her extension number, from which you can figure out the direct line.

Now you can use the old top-down approach: Call the manager's boss, who will probably refer you to the manager. But now when you call the manager, you say you've been referred by her boss, which will get you more respect.

How can I get past gate-keepers?

Start with a charm offensive on every gate-keeper (screener) you encounter. Leave confrontational behaviour to amateurs. Think of gate-keepers as human toggle switches that either pass you on to your target or off to oblivion.

Try the following phone techniques that have been worked out by legions of successful salespeople and recruiters since the telephone was invented:

> ✔ **Name identification:** When you don't know who the hiring decision-maker is, start simply by just asking a receptionist: 'I'm trying to locate your company's sales manager for West Sussex. Who is that, please?'

If the decision-maker's name is protected like a national security asset and you know the easily found extension for the sales department (ext. 123), call related extensions (121, 122, 124 and 125) and say to anyone who answers, 'Oh, I was trying to call the sales manager.' An employee untrained in the use of no-loose-talk scripts may tell you what you seek.

✔ **Readiness alert:** Be prepared to give a 30-second summary of who you are and your selling points for the target jobs in case the sales manager answers one of your calls.

Breaking through digital walls is easier when you realise that gate-keeping scripts don't vary much; almost all require your name, company and purpose of call before the gate-keeper decides what to do with you.

✔ **Ideal screen-buster:** The best tip is sailing in on the wings of a mutual acquaintance: 'This is John Jason. Tim Pitman, one of your boss's professional colleagues, thinks your boss and I should talk.' If coat-tail wings aren't available, bowl a googly into the gate-keeper's script and take charge of the conversation. Do it by interrupting her script. Sound confident. Use first names.

> You: *Good morning. To whom am I speaking?*

> Gate-keeper: *This is Lois.*

> You: *Lois, good morning. This is John Jason calling for David.*

> Effect: You interrupted the script! The gate-keeper may assume you work in the company or are an approved vendor and pass you on.

When you suspect a first-name-only approach is too cheeky for the situation, modify: 'Can I speak to David (small pause), David Wintergate?' If the gate-keeper asks you to repeat who is calling, use the same formula: 'John (small pause), John Jason.' The implication is that you know each other.

✔ **New good mate:** By being friendly, sincere, warm and humorous, and asking for help, you may convert the gate-keeper to an ally.

When asked why you're calling, skip phony reasons like: 'It's a personal matter.' That wheeze falls on deaf ears. Instead, research pays:

> *I understand that your boss has a mandate to cut costs. I've had serious experience with cost trimming, saving 10 per cent and more. I think he'd get value in speaking with me for a few minutes. I need your help in arranging to speak to David.*

The 'I'm here to help' approach allows the gate-keeper to present you as a solution to the hiring manager's problem, not as a pesky job hunter.

Similar to the patter you use with a central phone operator or receptionist, encourage your newfound mentor/ coach to name the best and worst times to call, how to pronounce the boss's name if it's unusual, and for the boss's email address. You're building rapport.

What can I do with voicemail?

When you can't break through voicemail, leave a short message showing upbeat interest, not desperation – and a time when you'll call back.

> *My name is Maureen Farmer – I'm calling you because I've successfully outgrown my job, and you have a reputation for running a progressive department. I think you have my CV. If you like what you see, can we talk? I'll call you tomorrow morning at 11:30 to arrange a convenient time.*

Pronounce your name clearly and say your telephone number at a moderate pace. Give the hiring manager a chance to write it down without replaying the message. Otherwise, the manager hears a 'garbledrushofwords' and decides 'Idon'thavetimeforthis', and moves on.

How often do you call? Some very smart experts suggest calling every five to ten days until you're threatened with arrest if you call again. But busy employers insist that – unless you're in sales or another field requiring a demonstration of persistence – after you're certain your CV was received, call one to two weeks later, and then no more than once every three to four weeks.

Although you don't want to become a pest, the volume of CVs in the New Era job market is turned up beyond rock-concert level. If your decision is between not being a pest or being ignored, lean towards more follow-up.

Following up by phone is your most effective tool, but you can, from time to time, substitute contacts by sending notes or email with additional facts about your qualifications, ideas to solve a problem you know the company is facing, a news clipping of mutual interest, or just an expression of your continuing interest in working for the company and the manager.

Why shouldn't I leave a message asking the target to call me back?

If you mess up your first voicemail call, it's a big mistake to leave your name and number and ask employers to call you back. Instead leave a very brief message indicating that you'll call again at a specific time. You may have to make a dozen calls before connecting, each time again giving a time frame for your next call. The trick is to

✔ Set a specific time and keep your word, which makes you look like a reliable person.

✔ Use phrases that prevent the target from feeling 'guilty' for missing your call after call. ('Please don't feel bad about missing my call. Afternoons may be better for you . . .')

How can I keep track of my follow ups?

You can fall back on the usual suspects: notebooks, card files, Excel or another computer spreadsheet program.

Alternatively, you can use a new web-based program called JibberJobber (www.jibberjobber.com), which at time of writing is free. JibberJobber allows you to enter information about your job search and not have to worry about how to set up or design the organisational system. You have to play around with it a little to get started, but you need not be technically minded.

When is it time to throw in the towel?

Suppose you do reach the hiring manager but you just can't close the interview invitation. Salvage something of your time and effort. Ask the 'Who should I call?' question. Does the manager, whom we'll name Barry Shore, know anyone at another good company who can gain by talking to you? You begin that call with a referral: 'Barry Shore at Top Ship suggested we might meet for a discussion of mutual benefit.'

Or suppose you never reach the hiring manager despite your dedicated effort. When is it time to say 'I've done all I can do and I'll explore other opportunities'? Move on perhaps after about 15 calls spread out over two months.

Monitoring Your Follow-up Efforts

When you've sent out a boatload of CVs and you're hardly, if ever, contacted for a job interview, you know it's time to re-examine your CV and make sure it's hitting the right angle, and when satisfied, power up your follow-up.

Now the big question becomes how much time you need to spend on each follow-up mission. You could make a trip to Mars faster than you can chase after all your CV submissions. You may even be thinking that the old 80/20 rule, which says only 20 per cent of your job search activities produce 80 per cent of results, applies to CV follow-up.

Figure 16-1 shows a CV Follow-Up Matrix. It's a tool you can use to make objective and comparative judgements about which CV submissions offer you the biggest returns for your time investments.

	Job 1	Job 2	Job 3	Job 4	Job 5
Your fit					
Company/Industry					
Salary/Benefits					
Training					
Location					
Personal Factors					

Total					

Figure 16-1: The CV Follow-Up Matrix.

The Matrix, which was created by James M. Lemke and John S. Gill, allows a simple, easy comparison of jobs for which you've thrown your hat in the ring. It spotlights the most promising jobs for you personally that you need to pursue quickly, and tags the less promising jobs that can wait until you have time on your hands.

Using the Follow-Up Matrix

The Follow-Up Matrix is divided into six main factors. The factors are divided into five value levels ranging from 0 to 4 (see the Values Key below). The values are based on the presumed quality of the position for which the CV was submitted.

You won't have all the information for each category. You may have to make some educated guesses. But if you follow the New Era strategy of customising your CV for each position, you have more than normal research at your fingertips.

The values inserted in each category of the Matrix are subjective. If you disagree with the examples, substitute your preferences to reflect your views about what's hot and what's not about any new position.

Additionally, you can change the point values in any category to suit yourself. If, for example, avoiding commuter stress is overwhelmingly important to you and you're willing to accept less in every other factor (like pay and training) for a job that's ten minutes from your residence, add 5 to 10 points to the neighbourhood job.

Factors on the Follow-Up Matrix

The following are some considerations that you may want to keep in mind when mulling over your options.

- ✔ **Fit:** How well do your qualifications align with the position's stated requirements? For example, if there are six requirements, how many can you match with qualifications?

- ✔ **Company/Industry:** Does the employer's focus reflect your own interests and culture? Is the company stable, an industry leader?

- ✔ **Salary/Benefits:** Does the pay package, if revealed, fit within your desired range? When you can't find out, award average points. Visit www.paywizard. co.uk or www.reed.co.uk/CareerTools/ SalaryCalculator.aspx to get an idea of what the position should pay.

- ✔ **Training:** Working with a progressive company that has the latest technology and generous training opportunities helps keep your skills up to date and marketable.

- ✔ **Location:** In your area, the time, stress and expense of commuting are factors. If you must move to another part of the country, consider relocation costs and who pays them, as well as the availability of housing and transport, and the quality of schools, recreational facilities and lifestyle.

- ✔ **Personal Factors:** Figure out what counts most with you and switch the values to conform to those things. Working mothers might choose to keep 'telecommuting and life/work fit' as the top value. Baby boomers might value 'flexible hours or part-time work'. It's your call.

TIP

If you sent a CV for a job that you give four points to in each of the six categories, that's 24 points and you need to run, not walk, to follow up on that winner. By contrast, if you sent a CV for a position that you give only one point to in each of the six categories, depending on what else is on your plate at the time, you may want to exert a minimum of effort to follow up on that loser.

The Values Key

Fill in each job's six factors using this key (feel free to change it if the values differ from your own).

Fit

0 = Not qualified at all, but I'm desperate

1 = I think I could do the job, but my CV says no

2 = I'm qualified but so are many others

3 = I'm very qualified so I should get noticed

4 = I'm extremely qualified and can make an immediate impact

Company/Industry

0 = No future/too many layoffs

1 = Steady/limited growth opportunities

2 = Solid performer

3 = Industry leader

4 = Cutting edge leader

Salary/Benefits

0 = Unemployment better option

1 = Beats unemployment

2 = Average

3 = Great

4 = Outstanding

Training

0 = Going nowhere job

1 = Little training/old technology

2 = Some training/current technology

3 = Good training/new technology

4 = Great training/new technology

Location

0 = Ghastly commute/unpaid relocation to a dump

1 = Each way 1 hour

2 = Each way 30-45 minutes

3 = Less than 30 minutes each way/frequent transport

4 = Home office, or paid relocation to paradise

Personal Factors

0 = Wrong culture

1 = Nice co-workers

2 = Fancy office

3 = Telecommuting

4 = Work/life balance

Checking out a sample Matrix

Figure 16-2 illustrates how the CV Follow-Up Matrix helps you allocate your follow-up time. Go after Job 2 and Job 3 immediately. Follow up on Job 5 and Job 1 when convenient. Don't waste your time on Job 4.

	Job 1	Job 2	Job 3	Job 4	Job 5
Your fit	0	4	1	1	2
Company/Industry	3	4	3	0	2
Salary/Benefits	0	4	4	3	3
Training	2	4	3	0	1
Location	2	4	2	0	1
Personal Factors	1	4	1	0	1
Total	8	24	14	4	10

Figure 16-2: Example of how you might use the CV Follow-Up Matrix.

Fast-Tracking Your Successful Follow-Up

Although following up does take an investment of your time, it need not suck all the oxygen from your life's free hours. The CV Follow-Up Matrix encourages smart time management while reminding you that good things no longer come to someone who waits.

Often the wait is longer than you expect. Many people think the recruitment cycle is about 30 to 45 days, when the actual figure is closer to 90 to 120 days, according to veteran job placement experts.

Any number of things delay decisive employment action: The first choice candidate backs out, employers change their priorities while dealing with a crisis, management freezes budgets, hiring managers go on holiday, or rumours surface of an impending merger, to name but a few.

Jobseekers who diligently follow up CV submissions sometimes discover that on their fifth or sixth call to a target company, seven or eight weeks later, the company's interviewing process has risen from the dead and is given new emphasis. There you are, metaphorically speaking, on the right street corner at the right time when the right bus comes along – and you get on the bus.

Chapter 17

Almost Got the Interview Date? Prepare Yourself

• •

In This Chapter

▶ Setting or rescheduling a mutually agreeable interview date

▶ Assuring 'same-room' interviews

▶ Showing enthusiasm without losing money

▶ Paying for travel to interviews

▶ Handling a rush of employer interest

• •

*S*o you've sent out your CV and been asked for an interview. Now it's merely a matter of the where and when. At this point, nothing can wreck your meeting. Or can it? The inconvenient answer is 'yes'.

Countless factors that are beyond your control – such as a sudden budget crunch that kills the position – can derail your run for promising interviews.

Fortunately, most of the accidents waiting to happen are small things you can control. Unfortunately, even small missteps can have a big bad impact. To make sure you don't snatch defeat from the jaws of victory, here are five illustrations of developments where little things mean a lot to your future.

When Your Job Conflicts with an Interview Date

You're employed, with a hectic job, which is one reason you want to make a getaway. A recruiter contacts you with an interesting offer of an interview with a hiring manager. The problem is the manager wants to meet with you during a busy workday.

If you have no holiday or other leave time available and you've replaced every tooth in your mouth, your best option is to propose an evening or weekend meeting so that you can comply with your honourable work ethic:

I am excited about meeting Harry Lucas but, in good conscience, I can't cheat my current company and take a workday off right now. My management is counting on me to complete a company-wide stock-take next week. Can we possibly set up an early evening meeting, say Tuesday or Wednesday?

If the employer says no to an early evening interview, suggest an interview around lunchtime.

Should an emergency arise at your present job requiring you to change an interview time, use the same approach – you're a conscientious employee and never let your team down. But remember, rescheduling an interview once is risky; twice is fatal.

Face-to-Face Beats Ear-to-Ear

Telephone interviews are actually *screening interviews* to find out whether you're worth the investment of time that a regular interview requires. You aren't going to be hired for a good job until you get in the same room with a person who has the authority to hire you. That's why even in a formal telephone interview with a screener you need to keep pushing for a face-to-face interview.

Whenever possible, avoid answering employment questions on a mobile phone; they have a propensity for audio mishaps. ('Can you hear me now?') Say you'll call right back on a landline.

Going Overboard on Ardour Can Cost You Money

Accepting an interview invitation is cause for celebration. So when you're making the interview arrangements, be friendly and agreeable, warm and pleasant, but also show a little restraint. Exhibiting thrilled, puppy-dog excitement and face-licking gratitude can plant the idea that you're desperate and willing to accept below-market-rate pay, as well as raise doubts about why you're desperate for new employment. Set up the interview appointment as though you're looking forward to it but not because you 'need' the job.

Zeal and youthful enthusiasm work well for young graduates but not so well for jobseekers over the age of 25. It's a negotiation issue.

When the Interview Is Out of Town

If a company contacts you and requires an out-of-town interview, the company should pick up the tab.

If you made the contact, the issue is murkier. A cool way to find out who will pay travel costs for you to get to a company-site interview is to fudge the issue. Here are two examples:

> *Should I contact your company's travel department or do you use an outside travel agent?*
>
> *Will your company be making the travel arrangements for me?*

If you're on your own for travel costs, your decision may be difficult. It helps if the interviewing location is in a pleasant spot and you can combine your trip with a little holiday (ask your tax adviser if the travel is deductible).

If you're a starving new graduate, you can get away with pleading poverty, saying you'd love to come and see them in a city far away but that you spent your last pound getting the quality education that qualifies you as a candidate for employment by the target company.

If employers don't state their policy on what they'll pay for, just ask.

Schools and non-profit organisations may have a policy requiring all candidates to pay their own interview travel expenses. Don't reject the interview invitation outright if you can't see how you'll afford the travel expenses in the near future. Accept it – you can always cancel later.

Take stock of your situation and determine whether you can make the trip work: Do you have a friend or family member who will welcome you as a guest? Can you get a cheap train fare? Can you double (or triple) up and find interviews with other prospective employers in the area?

Making the Most of Your Moment

You seem to be the candidate of the hour: Four companies are requesting your presence for an interview – all in the same week! What a happy dilemma, you say.

And it is, particularly because you can put yourself in the best position possible – and get a little interviewing practice – if you utilise the following strategy:

1. **Review the CV Follow-Up Matrix in Chapter 16.**

2. **Rank the four companies from one to four, with one being your top pick.**

3. **Accept interviews with numbers three and four first,
   and one and two last.**

Not only will you be in interviewing mode by the time you talk
with your top picks, but companies number three and four
may make you an offer that you can use to force a quicker
decision by your top choice.

Prioritise and set up your interviews quickly. If you don't
move fast enough to schedule an interview, an employer
who's impatient to fill the position may make a choice before
seeing you. It's unlikely, but possible.

Part V
The Part of Tens

'It says here you are artistic and have
a good knowledge of typefaces —
do you have any samples handy?'

In this part . . .

You see why the famous *For Dummies* Part of Tens is treasured for putting information quickly and simply on your table. Find out what really ticks off recruiters, and how to back up your claims. Plus, you get a detailed checklist you can use to score your own CV.

Chapter 18

More than Ten Ways to Prove Your Claims

In This Chapter

▶ Proving your accomplishments using ten number statements

▶ Documenting your claims using ten percentage statements

▶ Backing your results using ten pound-amount statements

So you have excellent communications skills, your meetings with people go well, and you can make a computer work magic. At least, that's what you assert. How can an employer believe you?

An employer is more likely to believe your claims of skills and accomplishments when you back them up with specifics. A good start on backing up your statements is *measuring* them with numbers, percentages and amounts in pounds. For example, compare the following statements in Column A with the statements in Column B. Which is the strongest, most attention-grabbing, most convincing?

Column A	Column B
Easy ways to be more popular	50 easy ways to be more popular
Towels on sale	Towels 40% off
Designed internal company insurance plan to replace outside plan at great savings	Designed £30 million personal health insurance plan, saving estimated £5 million per year over previous external plan

We think you'd agree that the Column B statements win hands down! The take-home message is *measure, measure, measure*. This chapter contains ten statements in three categories: numbers, percentages and amounts in pounds. Fill in the blanks as a reminder to measure your accomplishments and results.

Say It with Numbers

Using numbers to convince the employer that you can become a valuable asset to the company is often more effective than using adjectives.

If you say you have 'extensive experience in' something, you run the risk of not sounding as convincing as if you say you have 'more than 20 years' experience in' your field.

1. __ years of extensive experience in _____ and _____.

2. Won ____ awards for _____.

3. Trained/Supervised ____ full-time and ____ part-time employees.

4. Recommended by _____ (a number of notable people) as a _____ (something good that they said about you) for excellent _____ (an accomplishment or skill).

5. Supervised a staff of ____.

6. Recruited ____ staff members in _____ (period of time), increasing overall production.

7. Sold ____ number of products in _____ (period of time), ranking ____ (1st, 2nd, 3rd) in sales in a company of ____ employees.

8. Exceeded goals in __ years/months/days, establishing my employer as ____ (1st, 2nd, 3rd, or whatever number) in industry.

9. Missed only ___ days of work out of ____ total.

10. Assisted ____ (executives, supervisors, technical directors, others).

Say It with Percentages

Using percentages in your CV stimulates interest, especially if you're seeking a position in sales, marketing or retail management. Percentages show that you're capable of achieving targets.

Instead of writing 'Instrumental in business growth over a number of years', write 'Registered 70 per cent increase in contracts over two years'. The former is waffle, the latter is targeted!

1. Excellent_____ (your top proficiency) skills, which resulted in ____ (per cent) increase/decrease in _____ (sales, revenues, profits, clients, expenses, costs, charges).

2. Recognised as a leader in company, using strong skills to effect a/an ____ (%per cent increase in team/co-worker production.

3. Streamlined _____ (industry procedure), decreasing hours spent on task by ____ (per cent).

4. Used extensive _____ (several skills) to increase customer/member base by ____ (per cent).

5. Financed __ (per cent) of tuition/education/own business.

6. Graduated within the top ____ (per cent) of class.

7. Responsible for an estimated __ (per cent) of employer's success in _____ (functional area/market).

8. Resolved customer relations issues, increasing customer satisfaction by ____ (per cent).

9. Eliminated _____ (an industry problem), increasing productivity by ____ (per cent).

10. Upgraded _____ (an industry tool), resulting in ____ (per cent) increase in effectiveness.

Say It with Amounts in Pounds

Using specific amounts in your CV definitely attracts attention. For architects, project managers and people who reduce operational costs, providing cost information is ideal for competitiveness.

Instead of writing that you completed 'major international projects', state that you 'executed projects valued at minimum of £1.8 million'.

1. Supervised entire _____ (a department) staff, decreasing middle-management costs by ____ (amount).

2. Purchased computer upgrade for office, saving the company ____ in paid hours.

3. Eliminated the need for _____ (one or several positions in company), decreasing payroll by __.

4. Averaged ____ in sales per month.

5. Collected ____ in memberships and donations.

6. Supervised the opening/construction of new location, completing task at ____ (amount) under projected budget.

7. Designed entire _____ programme, which earned ____ in company revenues.

8. Implemented new _____ system, saving ____ daily/weekly/monthly/annually.

9. Reduced cost of _____ (substantial service) by developing and implementing a new _____ system at the bargain price of ____.

10. Restructured _____ (organisation/system/ product) to result in savings of ____.

Chapter 19

Ten Ways to Improve Your CV

In This Chapter

▶ Eliminating anything that doesn't support the job you're targeting

▶ Being clear around about what you're applying for

▶ Finding success in the five per cent rule

*T*hink your CV could sparkle with a few tweaks? You may be right. In this chapter, we suggest ten easy fixes to power up to targeted status.

Match Your CV to the Job

To dart past job software filters, a CV must closely meet the requirements in the job description. If you know what company recruiters are looking for, make sure you put it in the top quarter of your CV. If instead you're posting your CV in databanks, research the career field for typical requirements and include those that apply to you.

Use Bulleted Style for Easy Reading

Using one- or two-liners opens up your CV with white space, making it more appealing to read. Professional advertising copywriters know that big blocks of text suffocate readers. Let your words breathe! However, use bullets only when you're attaching them to single sentences across the page. And make sure not to use bold, heavy type or those bullets that look like helicopter rudders. By doing so you kill the CV!

Discover the Art of Lost Articles

Although using articles – 'a,' 'an' and 'the' – in your CV isn't *wrong,* try deleting them for a crisper and snappier end result. Recruiters and employers expect to read CVs in compact phrases, not fully developed sentences.

The first person 'I' is another word that your CV doesn't need. Look at the following examples:

With Articles	*Without Articles*
I report to the plant manager of the largest manufacturer of silicone-based waxes and polishes.	Report to plant manager of largest manufacturer of silicone-based waxes and polishes.
I worked as the only administrative person on a large construction site.	Worked as only administrative person on large construction site.

Sell, Don't Tell

Forget sticking to the old naming-your-previous-responsibilities routine. Merely listing 'Responsible for setting up exhibitions' doesn't assure the recruiter that you met your responsibility or that the result of your efforts was worth the money someone paid you. Instead, write 'Succeeded in registering more than 300 international delegates'.

By contrast, read over your CV and make sure you've answered that pesky 'So what?' question lying in ambush for each bit of information you mention. Try to imagine what's running through a recruiter's mind when you relate that you were responsible for XYZ: *So what? Who cares? What's in it for me?* Anticipate those questions and answer them before a recruiter has a chance to toss your CV into the bin. (Chapter 5 discusses this advice in more detail.)

Show Off Your Assets

Recruiters are wild about snaring the cream of the crop. If you're in the top five per cent of any significant group (graduation, sales, attendance record, performance ratings) make sure that fact appears prominently on your CV.

Make Sure Your Words Play Well Together

Old wisdom: Use a lot of action verbs to perk up reading interest in CVs (see Chapter 7). *Later wisdom:* Cash in some of the action verbs for nouns, the keywords that ward off anonymity in sleeping CV databases. *New wisdom:* Use both nouns and verbs.

Just don't mix noun and verb phrases in the same CV section. The following example shows what you don't want to do.

> ### *Highlights:*
>
> • Founded start-up, achieving positive cash flow and real profits in the first year. [verb]
>
> • President of point-of-sale products. [noun]
>
> • Proven ability for representation of high technology products. [noun]
>
> • Consistently achieved highest profit in 45-year-old company history. [verb]

Instead, change the noun statements to be consistent with the verb statements:

> • Served as president of point-of-sale products.
>
> • Proved ability to represent high-technology products.

This agreeable notion is called *parallel construction.*

Reach Out with Strength

Highlight the qualifications and past job activities that are relevant to the kind of job you want and the skills you want to use.

Don't muddle your CV's message with minor skills or skills you no longer wish to use; stay on message.

Avoid a Weak Skills Profile

Imagine an actor striding onto a stage, stopping, and then standing there like a log addressing the audience: 'I came to find out what you can do for me.'

Not exactly a curtain raiser any more than beginning your CV with simply awful objective statements like: 'Seeking a chance for advancement' or 'Wishing to utilise my skills'.

Retire trite messages like this one: 'To obtain a responsible job with challenging and rewarding duties'. Does someone out there really want an irresponsible position? One that's dull and unrewarding?

Be an editor! Draw a line through wussy wording that leaves everyone wondering whether you're a washout. Your statement can be simple yet effective: 'Management position in finance with more than ten years' experience of strengthening the bottom line.'

Check Out the Technology

Pick up the phone and call the HR department where you want to work and to which you're about to submit your CV. Ask: 'Before I send you my CV online, I want to check that you accept MS Word attachments?'

If the answer is *yes*, wrap fish and chips in that ugly ASCII plain text CV and throw it away, revelling in the fact that you can send the attractive version of your CV. If the answer is *no* – well, good try in this era of transition. After all, ugly is still better than unreadable.

Erase the 'Leave-Outs'

Eliminate clutter by removing useless information that doesn't support the reasons why you're a qualified candidate. Here's a short list of the worst offenders:

- Your NI number or driving licence number.

- The date your CV was prepared.

- Your company's telephone number.

- Your secondary school or grammar school if you're a university graduate.

- Dates you spent involved in university extracurricular activities.

- Dates you were involved with professional or civic organisations, unless using them to fill in gaps or add weight to your claims.

- Names of (human) past employers (put these on your reference sheet with contact information).

- Actual addresses of your previous workplaces.

- Names of your wives, husbands, children and ages. Just allude to the fact that you're married with two children. If you have limited space, cut this detail out. Well, unless you're applying to the Inland Revenue . . .

Chapter 20

Ten Things that Annoy Recruiters

In This Chapter

▶ Reading recruiters' inside talk

▶ Recognising irksome CV flaws

▶ Knowing when to overrule recruiters

C heck out what recruiters write when they think no 'civilians' (jobseekers) are reading. Both third-party (independent) recruiters and inside corporate recruiters share their thoughts freely on various Internet forums.

Here are ten categories of transgressions that various e-recruiters cite as making them grumpy.

CV-Free Pitches

I get annoyed when applicants email general questions without any CV instead of asking the questions and attaching a CV.

Always remember to attach a CV to your question.

Major Mismatches

I find it extremely annoying when people send CVs without reading our job description. If we advertise for a pizza chef, a bike mechanic is just as likely to nominate himself for the job, leaving us to figure out why. We don't have time for such speculation.

Our management positions require a background in a certain industry, plus experience. We get responses from people with one year of experience and no management background. We get CVs that claim their experience is ideal or that they read the position and found it to fit their skills exactly, when in reality they have none of the experience detailed in the job posting.

We advertised for a telecommunications consultant with call centre experience and received a CV of someone with experience in movie production and no experience in anything we were looking for. I am sure applicants would have a more positive outcome if they applied for positions that are relevant to their experience, although I doubt this situation will ever change.

Some jobseekers, particularly in technical fields, operate on the lottery theory and scatter CVs everywhere. A number of jobseekers adhere to the old-school 80 per cent strategy (if you fit 80 per cent of the job's requirements, give it a go) or believe that if you can manage one thing, you can manage anything.

Others seek ways to apply viable skills to new environments and, failing to make a strong enough case, are rejected because some recruiters are too inexperienced, overworked or insular to recognise the legitimacy of transitioning skills.

Still other jobseekers just don't get it and waste everyone's time in applying for jobs for which they're dramatically unqualified.

Solution: The targeted CV. (See Chapter 5.)

E-Stalking

One applicant emailed his CV and a few days later sent another, saying he was waiting for a response. I replied that we would contact him if we were interested. A few days later, and once a week for a few months, he sent emails that said only, 'Still waiting.' Creepy.

I would like to tell jobseekers to send only one CV. If you're 'open' to all appropriate positions, just say so!

Checking back periodically works best if you send new information of interest to the recruiter. You may send a relevant piece of information with a brief 'In case you missed this' note, adding that you continue to look forward to an interview at a time to suit the recruiter.

Saying that you're available for any appropriate position carries the risk that you're seen as too much of a generalist and expert at nothing, or desperate. If you do it, define the field: say 'appropriate position in accounting' or 'appropriate position in retail', for example.

Most applicant-tracking systems that companies are using now require jobseekers to create a login ID before permitting them to attach a CV. After you've logged into the company career site, you can easily modify a current CV, save multiple versions, and apply for multiple positions with the click of the mouse.

You may still be required to answer specific questions before a CV can be submitted for a specific job. If the questions are answered correctly (according to the company's standards), the recruiter or hiring manager is notified by email that a new qualified CV is available for review. If you don't pass the litmus test for qualification, your CV stays in the company's database and is searched on for future openings.

It doesn't stop the persistent applicant sending additional CVs or emails or making phone calls. The trick is not to become a pest.

Missing Caps and Typos

My sore spot is receiving emails with no use of capitalisation whatsoever, or with some words mysteriously capitalised and those that should be capitalised (proper names, beginning of a sentence) in lowercase.

For heaven's sake, use a spell-check. A neat CV will always be my preference over one that is not.

Every single book or article on CV writing we've ever seen recommends impeccable work. It would be a crying shame to put together a well-researched CV only to have it discarded because of misspellings and typos throughout the text.

Too Much Information

I give bad marks to people who think that sending their CV multiple times will increase their chance of getting a call for an interview. It won't.

I dislike it when the applicant puts several addresses in the 'to' email box and mass emails the CV. This unprofessional shortcut looks like no care is being taken in applying for each individual position.

Another practice to avoid is posting a hard copy of your emailed CV. Carry hard copies to an interview, but don't post or fax an additional copy – it's not necessary. As for emailing your CV, not only is it disrespectful to mass email your CV addressed to multiple names, but you don't want all those other people knowing where else you're applying for work.

Moreover, as the sea change of targeted CVs sweeps across the job market, the old-school 'blast' style mailings (one-size-fits-all) stand little chance of getting you into an interview room.

Date Grate

What annoys me is when jobseekers send CVs and don't specify start and end dates for jobs. As if this won't be at the top of my list to ask in an interview and a reference check – if they get to the interview process at all.

Always insert the dates you worked at a particular company, and the date you left. You don't have to write the month, just state the years. This guideline relates to jobs you've had in the previous ten years. If your work history goes back further, you can get away with summarising blocks of dates. For example: '1999–2010: Various teaching positions in . . .'

However, if jobs you did some time ago relate to the position you're applying for, re-edit the information and state the dates. Remember that the employer asks for two references, one from your current or more recent job, and one from any other job. If you believe a good reference will come from a not-so-recent job, you want the employer to realise that the job was substantial in terms of how many years you were in it.

Guess Who

It's a pain when I get incomplete CVs and covering letters without contact information. We have offices in several countries and a hotmail.com address doesn't suffice.

A pet peeve of mine is receiving CVs without the current employer listed. I can understand this in the case of web job site postings but when sending a CV to a specific employer, the current employer should be identified.

In response to the first comment, you can add to the 'hotmail. com' (or other free mailbox established for a job search) a P.O. box and a dedicated telephone answering service. That combination protects your privacy but makes it easy for a recruiter to contact you.

As for the second comment, you can use a generic description of your current position and skills, noting that you'll reveal the current employer's name in a job interview. We urge caution in fully revealing your identity and personal workplace information on the Internet.

File Style

I can't imagine why, but some people have to be told to submit a CV as a normal attachment in a common program (such as Word). I have received two-page Word documents as zip files! I have the software to handle zips, but many people do not.

Zip files are for documents the size of Manchester, not CVs. No one wants to bother unzipping, unless the recruiter's email program won't open Word files sent from your different email program, in which case zipping is the only answer.

Useless and Uninformative

I grow peevish when forced to read through fluff that does not relate to a workforce position. It doesn't matter to anyone in my office that you were the local beauty queen. It doesn't matter to anyone in my office, now you're 35, out of university and have held several jobs, that you attended a prestigious prep school. It doesn't matter to anyone in my office that your wife is the vice president of a well-known company.

Another thing that bugs me is the use of fancy graphics in CVs.

Stick to information related to your ability to do the job for which you're applying.

Probable Prevarication

I hate wasting my time on CVs from people who claim to have attended a school they never saw the inside of and to have worked for a company that they didn't.

Lying about a point of fact easily proved or disproved is riskier than ever in today's era of fact-checking background investigations. Recruiters and employers are getting wise to lies and are turning fib finding into a big business.

Despite the glib assurances from some that you must inflate your CV or else you'll be at a disadvantage because 'everybody's doing it', tall tales court trouble, as a number of high-placed executives have discovered on their way out the door.

Employers often assume that those who cheat on CVs and job applications also cheated at school and continue to do so in life.

Chapter 21

Your Ten-Point CV Checklist

In This Chapter

▶ Making sure your CV matches up with specific job qualifications

▶ Cleaning out messy CV errors

▶ Standing back for a fresh look at the impression you're making

▶ Trusting your CV skills but verifying overall results

*B*efore going public with your CV, give it a final walk-through. Tick the box in front of each item only when your CV meets the targeted standards. Give yourself 10 points for each tick. If you don't get a score of 100, go back to your keyboard and try again.

Matching Skills for Skills

❏ **You remember the new drive to customise CVs by matching your qualifications (skills, education) with the specific positions of a job, or by matching your qualifications with the expected qualifications in a career field.**

If you write a two-page CV, you remember to customise the first page, even if you do not customise the second page. (Chapter 1 discusses the customising requirement and why it's now important.)

Format and Style

❏ **You select the best format for your situation.**

For example, *reverse chronological* when staying in the same field, or *functional* when changing fields. (Chapter 5 covers CV formats.)

Focus and Image

❏ **You say what you want to do and why you should be interviewed to do it.**

You let your CV 'rest' for a day or so, and then look at it with fresh eyes. You consider its overall impression. What kind of 'brand' do you project? Your CV has a theme. You present yourself as focused – not merely desperate to accept just any job.

Achievements and Skills

❏ **You relate your skills to the skills needed for the job.**

You cite at least one achievement for each skill. You measure by using numbers, percentages or pound amounts for each achievement. You measure any statement you can. You highlight results, not just responsibilities. (For more on measuring, see Chapter 18.)

Language and Expressions

❏ **You make the most of your word choices.**

You use adequate keywords (nouns) to make your CV searchable. You use action verbs to put vitality in your CV. You eliminate words that don't directly support your bid for the job you want, as well as such meaningless words and phrases as 'References available'. You use industry jargon where appropriate, but you translate acronyms, technical jargon, or military lingo into easy-to-understand English. (Chapter 7 covers word usage.)

Content and Omissions

❏ **Your content supports your objective.**

You begin with either a skills summary or a job objective. Next, you state your experience. You begin with your education only if you're a new graduate with virtually no experience, or if your target job is related to education and training. You don't list personal information that isn't related to the job you seek, such as marital status, number of children, or height. (For tips on content, see Chapter 6.)

Length and Common Sense

❏ **You use a length that makes sense for the amount of information you're presenting.**

You limit your CV to one or two pages if you're lightly experienced, or two or three pages if you're substantially experienced. These page counts are only guidelines; your CV can be longer if necessary to put your qualifications in the best light. Additionally, your CV can exceed three pages if it's a professional CV. *Remember:* Don't jam-pack a jumble of text on one page; doing so makes your CV too difficult to read.

Appearance: Online Attached and Paper CVs

❏ **Your CV is a real looker.**

Your e-CV in a fully formatted Word document looks much like a fully formatted paper CV. You use an open layout with white space, minimum 2.5 centimetre margins, headings in bold typeface or capital letters, bullets, and other low-key graphic elements that make your CV look professional (see Chapter 8). Your paper CV is printed on white or eggshell paper, both for a business impression and because it may be scanned into a database.

Difficult Issues and Sugar-coating

❑ **You thoughtfully handle all problem areas, such as grouping irrelevant jobs, long-ago, part-time and temporary jobs.**

You account for all the gaps in the time frame of your CV. You scour your CV for possible hidden negatives and eliminate them as described in Chapter 10.

Proofreading and More Proofreading

❑ **Your CV contains no typos, no grammar disasters – no errors of any kind.**

You not only use your computer's spell-check, but you also double-check (and triple-check) it. You ask others to read it carefully. Typos are hot buttons to many employers – two errors and you're gone.

The Power of Targeted CVs

Most jobseekers don't understand how the innovative *Web 2.0* phenomenon is changing the way the Internet is connecting people with jobs.

That's why – after reading this book – you're ahead of your competition in understanding the variety of changes, including

✔ Employers' demands for precise matches of job requirements and your qualifications.

✔ Social networking and employee referral systems you can use.

✔ Blogs that carry targeted job ads for your interests and skill sets.

✔ RSS (Real Simple Syndication) feeds that sprint job openings to you immediately they're posted.

✔ Vertical job search engines that attempt to collect for
you every job opening in the universe.

Get a leg up by starting now at the beginning of a New Era in
job search. Plunge into writing your targeted core CV sooner
rather than later. You can't meet today's job market challenges relying on CV strategies from the past century.

Index

• A •

abbreviations, avoiding, 107
academic CV, 70–73
achievements, on checklist, 236
activities, on CV, 85
ad language, mirroring, 11
address, in contact details, 79
administration jobs
  buzz words for, 90
  keywords for, 102
age
  revealing negatively, 123
  targeted CVs by
    graduate with some experience,
      166, 168–169
    management, 166, 170–171
    school-leaver with no work
      experience, 165, 167
    senior executive, 166, 172–173
aggregators. *See* vertical job
      search engines
AIRS (website), 27
*AIRS Job Board and Recruiting
  Technology Directory,* 27
alignment pitfalls on ASCII CVs, 45
also, as poison word, 100
amounts in pounds, proving claims
  with, 222
analysis jobs
  buzz words for, 96
  case studies, 53
annual reports, finding keywords
  in, 105
appearance, on checklist, 237
applicant tracking system
  (ATS), 79

application forms
  about, 87, 137–138
  competency-based questions,
    143
  questions and answers, 139–143
  realities of, 138
  using a rough draft CV, 138–139
articles, avoiding using, 107, 224
ASCII (plain text) CVs
  about, 42–43
  converting CVs to, 43–44
  pitfalls, avoiding, 44–45
  sample, 43
assets, showing off, 224
assisted with, as poison words, 100
ATS (applicant tracking system), 79
attachments, 48, 233
awards, on CV, 86

• B •

banking jobs, keywords for, 102
behavioural assessment, as online
    screening component, 52
benefits, as factor on Follow-Up
    Matrix, 205, 206–207
blasting services (CV), pitfalls of,
    48–50
block letters, 111
BlogEasy (website), 37
Blogger (website), 37
Bloglines (website), 37
blogs, 36–37, 238
body, of cover letters, 149–150
bulleted styles, 114, 223–224
Butch Cassidy and the Sundance Kid
    (film), 59

buzz words
  about, 89–90
  for administration and
    management jobs, 90
  for financial management
    jobs, 98
  for helping and care work, 97
  for many skills, 99
  for maximum effect, 90
  for office support jobs, 94
  for research and analysis
    jobs, 96
  for sales and persuasion jobs, 92
  for teaching jobs, 95
  for technical ability jobs, 93

• C •

care work, buzz words for, 97
career field, targeted CVs by
  engineering, 162–163
  IT, 157–159
  management, 157–159, 166,
    170–171
  medicine, 182–183
career goals, in portfolio, 75
career objective, 78
case studies, 53, 133–137
central phone operators, 198–199
checking references, 189–190
checklist (CV), 235–239
civil service positions, 126–128
claims, proving
  about, 219–220
  with amounts in pounds, 222
  with numbers, 220
  with percentages, 221
closing salutations, 150
clutter, eliminating, 227
colour, 112
common sense, on checklist, 237
community sector CVs, 180–181
company, as factor on Follow-Up
  Matrix, 205, 206

company websites, job searching
  on, 28–30
competencies, on CV, 83–84
competency-based questions,
  139–143
components. *See* sections
considerations for follow-up
  central phone operators,
    198–199
  getting past gate-keepers,
    199–201
  messages, 202
  moving on, 203
  opening statement, 198
  phone or email, 197
  tracking, 202
  voicemail, 201–202
consistency, importance of,
  113–114
contact details, 78–80
contact media, in contact
  details, 80
content, on checklist, 237
converting CVs to plain text
  (ASCII), 43–44
core CVs, 13–18
cover letters
  about, 145, 148
  body, 149–150
  closing salutations, 150
  importance of, 145–146
  opening salutations, 148–149
  samples, 150–153
  types, 146–148
creating CVs
  about, 77–78
  focusing, 59–61
  formats
    about, 61–62
    academic CV, 70
    executive, 68–70
    multimedia, 62
    standard (reverse
      chronological), 62–65
    targeted, 66–68

video, 62
Web, 62
portfolio, 75–76
selling your CV, 57–59
speculative letter, 74
curriculum vitae. *See* CVs
customer service jobs, keywords
for, 103
customising spin-off CVs, 13
CV blasting services, pitfalls of,
48–50
CVs. *See also specific topics*
checklist, 235–239
generic compared with targeted,
7–9
in portfolio, 75

• *D* •

dates
conflicts for job interviews, 212
missing on CVs, 232–233
dismissed, as poison word, 100
Dixon, Pam (privacy theft), 49
drafting CVs for new graduates,
130–132

• *E* •

education
qualified teacher for jobs in,
176–177
section on CV, 82–83
e-forms, 46–47
80/20 rule, 203
eliminating clutter, 227
email
attachment etiquette, 48
follow-up, 197
subject lines, 47
employment summary for new
graduates, 135
engineering jobs, targeted CVs for,
162–163
e-portfolios, 62

e-stalking, 230–231
etiquette (attachments), 48
evaluation, as online screening
component, 52
EXE files, 48
executive format CVs, 68–70
experience level, targeted CVs by
graduate with some experience,
166, 168–169
management, 166, 170–171
school-leaver with no work
experience, 165, 167
senior executive, 166, 172–173
experience section, on CV, 82–83
expressions, on checklist, 236
eye-catching CVs, 47–48

• *F* •

Facebook (website), 33
face-to-face interviews, compared
with telephone interviews,
212–213
fast-tracking follow-up, 208–209
file attachments, 233
filtering job search results, 21
financial management jobs, buzz
words for, 98
Financial Times (newspaper), 29
finding references, 193–194
first-person pronouns, 106–107
fit, as factor on Follow-Up Matrix,
205, 206
focus
on checklist, 236
choosing, 123
CVs, 59–61
follow-up
about, 195, 203–204
central phone operators,
198–199
fast-tracking, 208–209
Follow-Up Matrix, 204–208
getting past gate-keepers,
199–201

follow-up *(continued)*
importance of, 195–196
messages, 202
moving on, 203
opening statement, 198
phone or email, 197
tracking, 202
voicemail, 201–202
Follow-Up Matrix
factors on, 205
sample, 204, 208
using, 204–207
Values key, 206–207
fonts
choosing size, 115–116
consistency in, 113
pitfalls on ASCII CVs, 45
Forman, Chris (CEO), 27
formats (CV)
about, 61–62
academic CV, 70–73
on checklist, 236
choosing, 126
executive, 68–70
multimedia, 62
standard (reverse
chronological), 62–65
targeted, 66–68
video, 62
Web, 62
forms (e-forms), 46–47. *See also*
application forms

● *G* ●

gate-keepers, 49, 199–201
general cover letter, 146–147
general job boards, 26
generic CVs, compared with
targeted CVs, 7–9
Gill, John S. (Follow-up Matrix
creator), 204
golden years
about, 115–116
lower-level jobs, 121–123

myths and realities, 119–121
pitfalls, avoiding, 123
returning after raising children,
124
strengths of maturity, 118
Google (website), 105, 126
graduates. *See* new graduates
grammar, 106–107

● *H* ●

helped with, as poison words, 100
helping jobs, buzz words for, 97
helping verbs, substituting, 107
help-wanted sections of
newspapers, 27–28
honours, on CV, 86
HTML CVs, 62
human resources jobs, keywords
for, 104

● *I* ●

icons, explained, 3–4
identity theft problems with CV
blasting, 49–50
image, on checklist, 236
impacted CV with focus sample, 60
improvements, making to CV,
223–227
Indeed (website), 24
industry, as factor on Follow-Up
Matrix, 205, 206
industry conference programmes,
finding keywords in, 105
information
giving too much, 232
missing, 233
useless and uninformative, 234
information technology jobs,
keywords for, 103
integrity tests, 53
interaction simulations, 53
Internet search engines, finding
keywords in, 105

Internet tools. *See* online tools
interviews, preparing for
about, 211
face-to-face or telephone,
212–213
job conflicts with date, 212
out-of-town, 213–214
prioritising, 214–215
restraint, showing, 213
in-tray exercises, 52
IT jobs, targeted CVs for, 157–159

• *J* •

James, Mark (career coach), 30
JibberJobber (website), 202
job boards, 25–27
job descriptions, finding keywords
in, 105, 106
job fairs, 126
job search tools
about, 39
CV blasting, negatives of
about, 48
overexposure to recruiters, 50
privacy and identity theft,
49–50
spam gatekeepers, 49
e-forms, 46–47
fully designed, eye-catching
documents, 47–48
matching CVs to jobs, 54
online screening
about, 50–51
pros and cons, 53
ranking CVs, 53–54
sample components of, 51–53
plain text CVs (ASCII)
about, 42–43
converting CV to, 43–44
pitfalls, avoiding, 44–45
scannable CVs, 39–42
'Job Seeker's Guide to CV: Twelve
CV Posting Truths,' 49
jobs, matching CV to, 223, 229–230

• *K* •

keywords
about, 100–101
for administration and
management jobs, 102
for banking jobs, 102
for customer service jobs, 103
defined, 89
for human resources jobs, 104
for information technology
jobs, 103
for manufacturing jobs, 104
poison words, avoiding, 100
where to find, 105–106
knowledge testing, as online
screening component, 52

• *L* •

language, 113, 236
lay-off, as poison word, 100
layout
about, 107
consistency, 113–114
font sizes, choosing, 115–116
length, 110
printing, 111–112
typefaces, choosing, 115–116
white space, 114–115
word processing, 110–111
lecturer sample cover letter, 152
Lemke, James M. (Follow-up Matrix
creator), 204
length of CVs, 110, 237
licences, on CV, 86
life phases
about, 115
from corporate to civil service,
126–128
golden years
about, 115–116
lower-level jobs, 121–123
myths and realities, 119–121
pitfalls, avoiding, 123

life phases *(continued)*
  returning after raising children, 124
  strengths of maturity, 118
  new civilian
    military strengths, 124–125
    myths and realities, 125–126
  temporary jobs, 127
live feeds, receiving. *See* RSS (Really Simple Syndication)
location, as factor on Follow-Up Matrix, 205, 207
long-winded sentences, 107
lower-level jobs, for golden years, 121–123
low-tech, appearing, 123
lying, 234

• M •

management jobs
  buzz words for, 90
  keywords for, 102
  qualified teacher for jobs in, 178
  targeted CVs for, 157–159, 166, 170–171
managerial assessments, as online screening component, 52–53
managing references
  about, 188, 194
  choosing, 190
  employers checking, 189–190
  omitting, 189, 191–193
  prompting, 190–191
  reference folder, 191
  thanking everyone, 193
manufacturing jobs, keywords for, 104
margins, 111
market forces, 11
mass posting in Web 1.0, 9–10
maturity, strengths of, 118
maximum effect, buzz words for, 91

medical jobs, targeted CVs for, 182–183
messages (follow-up), 202
Microsoft Word, 110–111
Microsoft Works, 111
military connections, in portfolios, 76
mirroring ad language, 11
missing caps, 231–232
missing information, 233
monitoring efforts of follow-up
  about, 203–204
  Follow-Up Matrix, 204–207
  sample Follow-Up Matrix, 204, 208
multimedia CVs, 62
MySpace (website), 32, 33
myths and realities
  golden years, 119–121
  new civilian, 125–126

• N •

name, in contact details, 79
name identification, using for follow-up, 199–200
National Insurance Number, 100
neutralising damaging references, 192
new civilian
  military strengths, 124–125
  myths and realities, 125–126
new graduates
  about, 127
  application forms
    about, 137–138
    competency-based questions, 143
    questions and answers, 139–143
    realities of, 138
    using a rough draft CV, 138–139
  case studies
    with experience, 133–135
    with no experience, 136–137

getting your foot in the door, 129–130
highlighting skills, 136
revising and drafting CVs, 130–132
sample cover letters, 151
sample CVs, 133–134, 137
with some experience, 166, 168–169
volunteer work, 131
work experience, 131
newspapers, 27–28
niche job boards, 26
not-for-profit sector jobs (website), 126
numbers, proving claims with, 220
Nurrenbrock, Mary (recruiter), 26

• *O* •

office support jobs, buzz words for, 94
omissions, on checklist, 237
online feeds, 20–21
online help-wanted ads, finding keywords in, 105
online profile sourcing, 35
online screening
about, 50–51
pros and cons, 53
ranking CVs, 53–54
sample components of, 51–53
online social networking
about, 33
features of, 33–34
getting started, 34–35
online profile, 35
online tools
company websites, 28–30
ease of using, 30
job boards, 25–27
newspapers, 27–28
overview, 19

vertical job search engines
about, 20
Indeed, 24
Reed, 25
signs of, 21
Simply Hired, 23
steps to using, 22–23
Totaljobs Group Ltd, 24–25
web searches for jobs, 20–22
opening salutations, 148–149
opening statements (follow-up), 198
organisation of this book, 2–3
organisations, on CV, 85–86
out-of-town interviews, 213–214
overexposure to recruiters, 50

• *P* •

paper, selecting, 112
passive 'being' verbs, 107
password-protected documents, attaching, 48
percentages, proving claims with, 221
personal factors, as factor on Follow-Up Matrix, 205, 207
personal information, for new graduates, 135
personality assessment, as online screening component, 52
persuasion jobs, buzz words for, 92
phone follow-up, 197
plain text CVs. *See* ASCII (plain text) CVs
planning case studies, 53
podcast (video), 62
poison words, avoiding, 100
portfolio, 75–76
pre-employment screening. *See* online screening
preparing core CV, as step to writing targeted CVs, 12

preparing for interviews
about, 211
face-to-face or telephone, 212–213
job conflicts with date, 212
out-of-town, 213–214
prioritising, 214–215
restraint, showing, 213
prescreening. *See* online screening
presentation exercises, 53
printed help-wanted ads, finding keywords in, 105
printing, 111–112
prioritising interviews, 214–215
privacy problems with CV blasting, 49–50
professional qualifications, for new graduates, 135
profiles (online), 35
proof of performance, in portfolios, 75
proof of recognition, in portfolios, 75
proofreading, on checklist, 238
proportional typefaces, pitfalls on ASCII CVs, 45
proving claims
about, 219–220
with amounts in pounds, 222
with numbers, 220
with percentages, 221
public sector jobs (website), 126

• *Q* •

questions, asking without attaching CVs, 229
questions and answers (application forms), 139–143

• *R* •

raising children, working after, 124
ranking CVs, 53–54

readiness alert, using for follow-up, 200
Really Simple Syndication. *See* RSS (Really Simple Syndication)
recruiters
overexposure to, 50
tips to avoid annoying, 229–234
reduction in force, as poison word, 100
Reed (website), 25
reference dossier, 191
references
about, 187
average, 1871–88
finding, 193–194
managing
about, 188, 194
choosing, 190
employers checking, 189–190
omitting, 189, 191–193
prompting, 190–191
reference folder, 191
thanking everyone, 193
references available, for new graduates, 135
references available upon request, as poison words, 100
relevancy, of jobs, 21, 226
research jobs, buzz words for, 96
research requirements, as step to writing targeted CVs, 12–13
responsibilities included, as poison words, 100
restraint, showing during interviews, 213
résumés. *See* CVs
reverse chronological (standard) CVs
about, 62–63
creating, 65
strengths and weaknesses, 64
who can use, 64–65
revising CVs for new graduates, 130–132

robots, 20
RSS (Really Simple Syndication)
  about, 37
  on checklist, 239
  features of, 38
  getting started, 38

• S •

salary, as factor on Follow-Up
    Matrix, 205, 206–207
salary history/requirements, 54, 88
sales jobs, buzz words for, 92
salutations, 148–149, 150
samples
  cover letters, 150–153
  Follow-Up Matrix, 204, 208
  graduate with experience, 133–134
  graduate with no experience, 137
  plain text (ASCII) CV, 43
  qualified teacher for jobs in
      education, 176–177
  qualified teacher for jobs in
      management, 178
  targeted CVs
    academic CV, 71–73
    community sector, 179
    core, 13–18
    for engineering field, 162–163
    executive format CVs, 69
    graduate with some experience,
        168–169
    impacted CV with focus, 60
    for IT field, 158–159
    for management field, 158–159,
        170–171
    for medicine field, 182–183
    overview, 13–18, 67
    school-leaver with no work
        experience, 167
    senior executive, 172–173
    specialist CV, 178–179
    spin-off CVs, 13–18
    standard (reverse
        chronological) CV, 63

samples of your work, in
    portfolios, 75
scannable CVs, 39–42
school-leaver with no work
    experience, 165, 167
screen-buster, 200
screening interviews, 212–213
Search4Blogs (website), 37
secondary school education, 123
sections. *See also* application forms
  about, 77–78
  activities, 85
  competencies, 83–84
  contact details, 78–80
  education, 82–83
  experience, 82–83
  honours and awards, 86
  key skills, 80–81
  licenses and work samples, 86
  organisations, 85–86
  salary, 88
selling your CV, 57–59, 224
senior executive, 166, 172–173
senior manager sample cover
    letter, 153
shifting tenses, 107
showing off assets, 224
Simply Hired (website), 23
skills
  avoiding weak profiles, 226
  buzz words for many, 99
  on checklist, 235, 236
  highlighting for new
      positions, 122
  key, 80–81
  turning irrelevant employment
      into, 136
skills testing, as online screening
    component, 52
social networking
  about, 33
  on checklist, 238
  features of, 33–34
  getting started, 34–35
  online profile, 35

sourcing (online profile), 35

spam gatekeepers, 49

spamming, consequences of, 10

special circumstances, targeted CVs for

community sector, 180–181

medical positions, 182–183

qualified teacher for jobs in education, 176–177

qualified teacher for jobs in management, 178

specialists, 178–179

specialist CVs, 178–179

specialty job boards, 26

specific cover letter, 147

speculative letter, 74

spell-check, 108, 231–232

spiders, 20

spin-off CVs, 13–18

standard (reverse chronological) CVs

about, 62–63

creating, 65

strengths and weaknesses, 64

who can use, 64–65

style, on checklist, 236

subject line, of emails, 47

submitting CVs in Web 2.0, 11–12

sugar-coating, on checklist, 238

• T •

tabs pitfalls on ASCII CVs, 45

tabulation settings, consistency in, 113

targeted CVs

about, 66

by age

graduate with some experience, 166, 168–169

management, 166, 170–171

school-leaver with no work experience, 165, 167

senior executive, 166, 172–173

by career field

engineering, 162–163

IT, 157–159

management, 157–159

medicine, 182–183

compared with generic CVs, 7–9

creating, 68

by experience level

graduate with some experience, 166, 168–169

management, 166, 170–171

school-leaver with no work experience, 167

senior executive, 172–173

power of, 238–239

samples, 13–18. *See also specific types*

for special circumstances

community sector, 180–181

medical positions, 182–183

qualified teacher for jobs in education, 176–177

qualified teacher for jobs in management, 178

specialists, 178–179

steps to writing, 12–13

strength and weaknesses, 66–67

who can use, 67–68

teaching jobs, buzz words for, 95

technical ability jobs, buzz words for, 93

technology

about, 226

alternative strategies to, 18

rapidly changing, 33

telephone interviews, compared with face-to-face interviews, 212–213

telephone number, in contact details, 79–80

temporary employment, 61, 127

tenses, shifting, 107

thanking referees, 193

tools (online)

company websites, 28–30

ease of using, 30

job boards, 25–27
newspapers, 27–28
overview, 19
vertical job search engines
  about, 20
  Indeed, 24
  Reed, 25
  signs of, 21
  Simply Hired, 23
  steps to using, 22–23
  Totaljobs Group Ltd, 24–25
  web searches for jobs, 20–22
Totaljobs Group Ltd (website), 24–25
tracking follow-ups, 202
trade magazines, finding keywords in, 105
training, as factor on Follow-Up Matrix, 205, 207
Twitter (website), 33
typefaces, 45, 115–116
Typepad (website), 37

• U •

useless and uninformative information, 234

• V •

value proposition, 17
Values key (Follow-Up Matrix), 206–207
verbs, helping, 107
vertical job search engines (VJSEs)
  about, 20
  on checklist, 239
  Indeed, 24
  Reed, 25
  signs of, 21
  Simply Hired, 23
  steps to using, 22–23
  Totaljobs Group Ltd, 24–25
  web searches for jobs, 20–22
video CVs, 62

video podcast, 62
VJSEs. *See* vertical job search engines
voice, using your own, 106
voicemail, for follow-up, 201–202
volunteer work, 131

• W •

Web 1.0, mass posting of CVs in, 9–10
Web 2.0
  evolving technology of, 32
  features of, 31–33
  submitting CVs in, 11–12
  web-based services of, 10–11
Web CVs, 62
web logs, 36–37
Web searches, 20–22
websites
  AIRS, 27
  BlogEasy, 37
  Blogger, 37
  Bloglines, 37
  compensation information, 54
  Facebook, 33
  Financial Times, 29
  Google, 105, 126
  Indeed, 24
  JibberJobber, 202
  job searching on company, 28–30
  MySpace, 33
  public and not-for-profit sector jobs, 126
  Reed, 25
  Search4Blogs, 37
  Simply Hired, 23
  Totaljobs Group Ltd, 24–25
  Twitter, 33
  Typepad, 37
  World Privacy Forum, 49
white space, 114–115
Wikipedia, 32
Word (Microsoft), 110–111
word processing, 110–111

word wrap pitfalls on ASCII CVs, 45
wording
  buzz words
    about, 89–90
    for administration and
      management jobs, 90
    for financial management
      jobs, 98
    for helping and care work, 97
    for many skills, 99
    for maximum effect, 91
    for office support jobs, 94
    for research and analysis
      jobs, 96
    for sales and persuasion
      jobs, 92
    for teaching jobs, 95
    for technical ability jobs, 93
  grammar, 106–107
  keywords
    about, 100–101
    for administration and
      management jobs, 102
    for banking jobs, 102
    for customer service jobs, 103
    for human resources jobs, 104
    for information technology
      jobs, 103
    for manufacturing jobs, 104
    poison words, avoiding, 100
    where to find, 105–106
  missing caps, 231–232
  spelling, 108, 231–232
  tips for, 225
WordStar, 111
work experience, 131
work samples, on CV, 86
worked with, as poison words, 100
Works (Microsoft), 111
World Privacy Forum (website), 49
Writing. *See also specific topics*
  cover letters
    about, 148
    body, 149–150
    closing salutations, 150
    opening salutations, 148–149
  targeted CVs, 12–13

Yahoo Finance, 29
YouTube, 32

• Z •

Zip files, 48, 233

UK editions

BUSINESS

Marketing Kit For Dummies
978-0-470-74490-1

Business Plans Kit For Dummies
978-0-470-74381-2

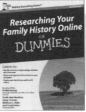

PRINCE2 For Dummies
978-0-470-71025-8

REFERENCE

British Politics For Dummies
978-0-470-68637-9

DIY For Dummies
978-0-470-97450-6

Researching Your Family History Online For Dummies
978-0-470-74535-9

HOBBIES

Growing Your Own Fruit & Veg For Dummies
978-0-470-69960-7

Allotment Gardening For Dummies
978-0-470-68641-6

Electronics For Dummies
978-0-470-68178-7

Anger Management
For Dummies
978-0-470-68216-6

Asperger's Syndrome
For Dummies
978-0-470-66087-4

Boosting Self-Esteem
For Dummies
978-0-470-74193-1

British Sign Language
For Dummies
978-0-470-69477-0

Cricket For Dummies
978-0-470-03454-5

Diabetes For Dummies,
3rd Edition
978-0-470-97711-8

Emotional Healing
For Dummies
978-0-470-74764-3

English Grammar
For Dummies
978-0-470-05752-0

Flirting For Dummies
978-0-470-74259-4

Football For Dummies
978-0-470-68837-3

Healthy Mind & Body All-in-One
For Dummies
978-0-470-74830-5

IBS For Dummies
978-0-470-51737-6

Improving Your Relationship
For Dummies
978-0-470-68472-6

Nutrition For Dummies,
2nd Edition
978-0-470-97276-2

**Available wherever books are sold. For more information or to order direct
go to www.wiley.com or call +44 (0) 1243 843291**

24940 (p1)

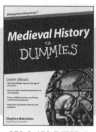

FOR DUMMIES®

The easy way to get more done and have more fun

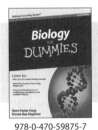
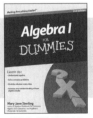

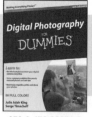
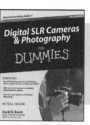